AF173939

Of Thee I Sing

A Musical in Two Acts

Book by George S. Kaufman & Morrie Ryskind

Music by George Gershwin

Lyrics by Ira Gershwin

A SAMUEL FRENCH ACTING EDITION

SAMUEL FRENCH

FOUNDED 1830

SAMUELFRENCH.COM

Copyright © 1931 by New World Music Corporation. Copyright © 1931, 1932 by George S. Kaufman and Morrie Ryskind. Copyright © 1958 (In Renewal) by Arthur Gershwin, Frances Godowsky, and Ira Gershwin. Copyright © 1958 (In Renewal) & 1959 (In Renewal) by George S. Kaufman. Copyright © 1963 (In Renewal) by Anna Kaufman Schneider. Copyright © (Acting Edition) by George S. Kaufman and Morrie Ryskind.

ALL RIGHTS RESERVED

CAUTION: Professionals and amateurs are hereby warned that *OF THEE I SING* is subject to a Licensing Fee. It is fully protected under the copyright laws of the United States of America, the British Commonwealth, including Canada, and all other countries of the Copyright Union. All rights, including professional, amateur, motion picture, recitation, lecturing, public reading, radio broadcasting, television and the rights of translation into foreign languages are strictly reserved. In its present form the play is dedicated to the reading public only.

The amateur live stage performance rights to *OF THEE I SING* are controlled exclusively by Samuel French, Inc., and licensing arrangements and performance licenses must be secured well in advance of presentation. PLEASE NOTE that amateur Licensing Fees are set upon application in accordance with your producing circumstances. When applying for a licensing quotation and a performance license please give us the number of performances intended, dates of production, your seating capacity and admission fee. Licensing Fees are payable one week before the opening performance of the play to Samuel French, Inc., at 45 W. 25th Street, New York, NY 10010.

Licensing Fee of the required amount must be paid whether the play is presented for charity or gain and whether or not admission is charged.

Stock/professional licensing fees quoted upon application to Samuel French, Inc.

For all other rights than those stipulated above, apply to: Samuel French, Inc., at 45 W. 25th Street, New York, NY 10010.

Particular emphasis is laid on the question of amateur or professional readings, permission and terms for which must be secured in writing from Samuel French, Inc.

Copying from this book in whole or in part is strictly forbidden by law, and the right of performance is not transferable.

Whenever the play is produced the following notice must appear on all programs, printing and advertising for the play: "Produced by special arrangement with Samuel French, Inc."

Due authorship credit must be given on all programs, printing and advertising for the play.

RENTAL MATERIALS

An orchestration consisting of **Piano/Conductor/Rehearsal Score, Reed 1 (Piccolo, Flute, Alto Sax, Clarinet), Reed 2 (Flute, Alto Sax, Clarinet), Reed 3 (Oboe, English Horn), Violin 1, Violin 2, Violin 3, Cello, Bass (Fendor/Acc.), Trumpet 2, Trombone, Drums** is available upon licensing from Samuel French. Contact Samuel French for perusal of the music materials as well as a performance license application.

No one shall commit or authorize any act or omission by which the copyright of, or the right to copyright, this play may be impaired.

No one shall make any changes in this play for the purpose of production.

Publication of this play does not imply availability for performance. Both amateurs and professionals considering a production are strongly advised in their own interests to apply to Samuel French, Inc., for written permission before starting rehearsals, advertising, or booking a theatre.

No part of this book may be reproduced, stored in a retrieval system, or transmitted in any form, by any means, now known or yet to be invented, including mechanical, electronic, photocopying, recording, videotaping, or otherwise, without the prior written permission of the publisher.

ISBN 978-0-573-68037-3   Printed in U.S.A.   #801

"OF THEE I SING"

STORY OF THE PLAY

The story follows John P. Wintergreen's campaign for President through until his triumphant election on the slogan "Put ove In the White House." As the chairman explained, "Wh : you need for an issue is something that everybody can get excited about and yet something that does not really make any difference." It is decided the candidate shall marry the winner of a beauty contest after proposing to her in every state in the Union. Wintergreen, however, falls in love with the pretty and demure Mary Turner instead. All this causes international complications.

Interwoven in the play are the comic adventures of Alexander Throttlebottom, the new Vice President, seeking recognition.

This play was awarded the Pulitzer Prize.

THE MUSIC BOX

SAM H. HARRIS AND IRVING BERLIN,
MANAGERS

PROGRAM · PUBLISHED · BY · THE · NEW · YORK · THEATRE · PROGRAM · CORPORATION

FIRE NOTICE: Look around now and choose the nearest exit to your seat. In case of fire, walk (not run) to that exit. Do not try to beat your neighbor to the street.

JOHN J. DORMAN, Fire Commissioner.

SAM H. HARRIS

PRESENTS

"OF THEE I SING"

A NEW MUSICAL COMEDY

BOOK BY GEORGE S. KAUFMAN and MORRIE RYSKIND
MUSIC BY GEORGE GERSHWIN
LYRICS BY IRA GERSHWIN

WITH

| WILLIAM | LOIS | VICTOR |
| GAXTON | MORAN | MOORE |

BOOK STAGED BY GEORGE S. KAUFMAN
SINGING AND DANCING ENSEMBLES STAGED BY GEORGIE HALE
SETTINGS BY JO MIELZINER
ORCHESTRA UNDER THE DIRECTION OF CHARLES PREVIN

Copy of program of first performance of "Of Thee I Sing," as produced by Sam H. Harris at The Music Box, New York:

CAST OF CHARACTERS

Louis Lippman .... *Sam Mann*
Francis X. Gilhooley .... *Harold Moffet*
Maid .... *Vivian Barry*
Matthew Arnold Fulton .... *Dudley Clements*
Senator Robert E. Lyons .... *George E. Mack*
Senator Carver Jones .... *Edward H. Robins*
Alexander Throttlebottom .... *Victor Moore*
John P. Wintergreen .... *William Gaxton*
Sam Jenkins .... *George Murphy*
Diana Devereaux .... *Grace Brinkley*
Mary Turner .... *Lois Moran*
Miss Benson .... *June O'Dea*
Vladimir Vidovitch .... *Tom Draak*
Yussef Yussevitch .... *Sulo Hevonpaa*
The Chief Justice .... *Ralph Riggs*
The Scrubwoman .... *Leslie Bingham*
The French Ambassador .... *Florenz Ames*
Senate Clerk .... *Martin Leroy*
Guide .... *Ralph Riggs*
Photographers, Policemen, Supreme Court Justices, Secretaries, Sightseers, Newspapermen, Senators, Flunkeys, Guests, *Etc.*

DESCRIPTION OF CHARACTERS

LIPPMAN: *An alert, rather good-looking Jewish politician. Aged about 40.*

GILHOOLEY: *A plausible Irish politician. Aged about 50.*

FULTON: *A very stout, florid man with gray hair. Aged 50.*

LYONS: *A medium-sized Southerner with mustache and goatee. Aged 60.*

JONES. *Tall, affable, white-haired and impressive. Aged 60.*

THROTTLEBOTTOM: *A short, cherubic, harmless little man—wistful in manner and expression. Aged 55.*

WINTERGREEN: *A good-looking, magnetic young man. Aged 30.*

JENKINS: *Young, snappy, black-haired. Aged 25.*

DIANA: *Tall, stately, beautiful and haughty. Aged 23.*

MARY: *A charmingly pretty, petite little girl. Aged 20.*

FRENCH AMBASSADOR: *A fiery little Frenchman. Aged 50.*

Of Thee I Sing

ACT ONE

SCENE I

(WARN Blackout.)

ARC LIGHTS up.

A campaign parade, staged down front in one. The background is a street drop, and across it is flung a huge election banner. It reads: "FOR PRESIDENT, JOHN P. WINTERGREEN. FOR VICE PRESIDENT, ALEXANDER THROTTLEBOTTOM." *The bottom of the banner is so wrinkled, however, that the name* THROTTLEBOTTOM *is not legible. Huge, out-of-focus pictures of the two candidates are also on the banner. It is night, and the paraders carry flares, red lights and noise-making machines. Each second or third person carries a sign—probably of the box variety, and lit from the inside so that the lettering may be easily read. The signs read as follows:*

"EVEN YOUR DOG LIKES JOHN P. WINTERGREEN"
"THE PEOPLE'S CANDIDATE"
"DON'T WASTE YOUR VOTE"
"TURN THE REFORMERS OUT"
"HAWAII WANTS WINTERGREEN"
"HE'S GOOD ENOUGH FOR ME"
"VOTE FOR PROSPERITY AND SEE WHAT YOU GET"
"WINTERGREEN—A MAN'S MAN'S MAN"
"THE FULL DINNER JACKET"
"WINTERGREEN LOVES YOU"
"HE KEPT US OUT OF JAIL"
"NEXT STOP THE WHITE HOUSE"
"WINTERGREEN—THE FLAVOR LASTS"
"A VOTE FOR WINTERGREEN IS A VOTE FOR WINTERGREEN"
"WIN WITH WINTERGREEN" (8 *or* 10 *of these*)
"WINTERGREEN FOR PRESIDENT (8 *or* 10 *of these*)

9

There are about fifty in the parade. They march around three times, stopping the third time and facing the audience. The MUSIC is "WINTERGREEN FOR PRESIDENT"—a song which includes bits of old campaign tunes. They march off and the LIGHTS black out.

BLACKOUT.

ACT ONE

SCENE II

When drop is up, stage and ARC LIGHTS.

The Scene is a hotel bedroom. Hall door down on R., bathroom door L. Bed up R. Telephone table at head of bed on R. side; suitcase bench at foot of bed. Table and chair L. Chairs down R. and down L.

Ingredients for drinks on table—glasses, White Rock, whiskey. Lolling on the bed, shirt-sleeved and reading a newspaper, LOUIS LIPPMAN; sitting at the table, leisurely playing solitaire, is FRANCIS X. GILHOOLEY.

GILHOOLEY finishes his game, leans back in his chair, repeats the last phrase of the parade music. LIPPMAN puts down his paper; sings. A KNOCK on the R. door.

CHAMBERMAID. *(Enters R., carrying towels. Crossing to bathroom L.)* I brought you some towels. *(PHONE rings. To GILHOOLEY, as she passes him)* I'm just going to the bathroom.

GILHOOLEY. First door to the left. (MAID *disappears into bathroom as* LIPPMAN *answers phone.)*

LIPPMAN. So what? Who? What's his name? Throttle *what?* Must have the wrong room. This is the National Committee. I say this is the National Campaign Committee. *(Hangs up)* Some fellow downstairs. (CHAMBERMAID *re-enters, crosses to L. of bed.)*

GILHOOLEY. Did you find it?

CHAMBERMAID. Shall I turn the bed down now?

LIPPMAN. Sure. Go ahead.

CHAMBERMAID. I can't turn it down unless you get off it

LIPPMAN. Oh, then the hell with it!

CHAMBERMAID. Yes, sir. *(Crossing to door* R.*)* Shall I come back later? *(At door.)*

LIPPMAN. Why not?

CHAMBERMAID. Yes, sir. *(Exits* R.*)*

LIPPMAN. Nice girl.

GILHOOLEY. *(Rising and stretching. Crosses to foot of bed)* Ho-hum! Certainly is great to take it easy for a while.

LIPPMAN. Yep. It was a tough convention, all right.

GILHOOLEY. I'll say it was tough. Sixty-three ballots.

LIPPMAN. But we put the ticket over. That's the big thing.

GILHOOLEY. Well, there's still the election. I don't mind telling you I'm a little bit worried.

LIPPMAN. Say, we never lost an election yet, and we've had a lot worse candidates.

GILHOOLEY. It ain't just the candidates—it's the whole party.

LIPPMAN. What do you mean the whole party?

GILHOOLEY. Mm. I think maybe they're kind of getting wise to us.

LIPPMAN. Say! If they haven't got wise to us in forty years, they'll never get wise.

GILHOOLEY. Yah, but I don't like the way they've been acting lately. You know, we never should have sold Rhode Island.

LIPPMAN. What are you worrying about? We've got a great ticket, haven't we? For President: John P. Wintergreen. He even *sounds* like a President.

GILHOOLEY. That's why we picked him. *(Crossing* L.*)*

LIPPMAN. Yes—and for Vice-President— *(Hesitates)* Say —what's the name of that fellow we nominated for Vice-President?

GILHOOLEY. *(Eases* C. *a bit)* Ah—Pitts, wasn't it?

LIPPMAN. No, no—it was a longer name.

GILHOOLEY. Barbinelli?

LIPPMAN. No.

GILHOOLEY. Well, that's longer.

LIPPMAN. You're a hell of a National Committeeman. Don't even know the name of the Vice-President we nominated.

(MATTHEW ARNOLD FULTON *enters* R.*; crosses to* C. *The* OTHERS *greet him.)*

FULTON. Hello, Louis; hello, Frank.

LIPPMAN. Hey, Fulton, to decide a bet: What's the name of that fellow we nominated for Vice-President?

FULTON. *(Foot of bed)* What? Oh—Schaeffer, wasn't it?

GILHOOLEY. That's right.

LIPPMAN. No, no! Schaeffer turned it down.

GILHOOLEY. Wait a minute! Wait a minute! Are you sure we nominated a Vice-President?

FULTON. Of course. Didn't I make the nominating speech? What was his name again?

GILHOOLEY. Well, think a minute. How did you come to nominate him?

LIPPMAN. Who introduced him to you?

(Together)

FULTON. Nobody introduced him. I picked his name out of a hat. We put a lot of names in a hat, and this fellow lost. *(PHONE rings. GILHOOLEY crosses L. to table.)*

LIPPMAN. *(At phone)* Hello. No, no, you've got the wrong room. What's his name again? Gotabottle? Oh, Throttlebottom. Wait a minute. *(To OTHERS)* Guy named Bottlethrottle says he has an appointment with somebody here.

FULTON. *(Sitting)* Never heard of him.

GILHOOLEY. Not me. *(Crosses to L. of table—gets cigar.)*

LIPPMAN. *(Into phone)* Must have the wrong room. Tell him this is the National Committee. Well, then, tell him it isn't the National Committee. Hello. And give me Room Service, will you?

(Together)

GILHOOLEY. *(Lighting a cigar)* What do you know, Matty?

FULTON. *(Crossing to table)* I know I'm thirsty.

GILHOOLEY. Got just the ticket. *(Getting bottle from under table.)*

FULTON. Had it analyzed?

GILHOOLEY. Had it psycho-analyzed. *(At table with drink.)*

LIPPMAN. Room Service? This is four hundred and thirteen. Listen—send up a half a dozen bottles of White Rock, a couple of ginger ales— *(To OTHERS)* Who's paying for this?

GILHOOLEY. General party expense.

LIPPMAN. *(Into phone)* Make that a dozen ginger ales. And some dill pickles. *(Hangs up)* Well, Matty, how's the newspaper king?

FULTON. Well, if you want to know, a little bit worried.

LIPPMAN. What's the matter?

FULTON. Well, I've just been over to the office doing some long-distance phoning. Called up about twenty of my editors all over the country, and it's not going to be the cinch we figured on.

GILHOOLEY. *(To* LIPPMAN*)* What did I tell you?   *(Together)*

LIPPMAN. What did you find out?

FULTON. Just that. It isn't going to be the cinch we—

(SENATORS CARVER JONES *and* ROBERT E. LYONS *enter* R. SENATOR JONES *is from the West, and* SENATOR LYONS *is from the South. Crossing* C. LYONS *shakes hands with* GILHOOLEY. JONES C.*)*

JONES. *(Oratorical in manner)* Ah, gentlemen, good evening!

LYONS. Good evening, gentlemen!   *(Together)*

GILHOOLEY. Hello, Senator!

LIPPMAN. Senator!

FULTON. How about Wintergreen? Is he coming over?

JONES. (R.C.) My friends, I am informed on excellent authority that John P. Wintergreen will shortly honor us with his presence. *(Crosses* R. *to bed—sits on trunk rack at foot of bed.)*

FULTON. Fine! Gentlemen, you probably wonder why I asked you over here.

LYONS. *(Sighting the liquor and pouring a drink)* Something about a drink, wasn't it?

FULTON. Senator Jones—

JONES. *(At once the orator—rises, crossing to* R.C.*)* My friends—

FULTON. Senator Jones—

JONES. My good friends—

FULTON. You're a man that keeps his ear close to the ground. What do they think about the ticket in the West?

JONES. My very good friends— *(Clearing his throat)* John P. Wintergreen is a great man—one of the greatest that the party has nominated since Alexander Franklin—

LYONS. *(Drops down* C.*)* And Robert E. Lee—

JONES. Unfortunately, however, while the people of the West admire our party, and love our party, and respect our party, they do not trust our party. And so, gentlemen, in the name of those gallant boys who fought overseas, and the brave mothers who sent them, we must not, we can not, we dare not allow Russian Bolshevism to dump cheap Chinese labor on these free American shores! Gentlemen, I thank you. *(Finishes his drink, hands glass to* LIPPMAN *for refilling, sits on trunk rack.)*

FULTON. Thank *you,* sir. And now, Senator Lyons, tell us about the South.

LYONS. (C. *Puts glass on table*) Gentlemen, you ask me about the South. It is the land of romance, of roses and honeysuckle, of Southern chivalry and hospitality, fried chicken and waffles, salad and coffee.

LIPPMAN. No dessert? (LYONS *reacts—goes to table and takes drink.*)

FULTON. Thank you, gentlemen. That just about confirms what my editors have been telling me. The people of this country demand John P. Wintergreen for President, and they're going to get him whether they like it or not. And, between you and me, gentlemen, I don't think they like it. (*A KNOCK on R. door.*) Come in.

(*Door R. is slowly opened. ALEXANDER THROTTLEBOTTOM enters—hopefully and timidly smiling.*)

THROTTLEBOTTOM. Good evening, gentlemen.

FULTON. Yes, sir. What can we do for you?

THROTTLEBOTTOM. Good evening—Mr. Fulton.

FULTON. (ALL *rise*) I'm afraid I don't quite place you. Your face is familiar, but— (GILHOOLEY *crosses to* THROTTLEBOTTOM.)

THROTTLEBOTTOM. I'm Throttlebottom. (*Crossing R.C.*)

FULTON. What?

THROTTLEBOTTOM. Alexander Throttlebottom.

JONES. (ALL *pushing him out backwards*) We're very busy, my good man. If you'll just—

THROTTLEBOTTOM. But I'm Throttlebottom.

FULTON. I understand, Mr. Teitelbaum, but just at present—

GILHOOLEY. You come back later on.

LIPPMAN. After we're gone.

(Together)

THROTTLEBOTTOM. But I'm Throttlebottom. I'm the candidate for Vice-President. (*General ad lib. greeting.*)

FULTON. That's the fellow!

GILHOOLEY. Of course!

LIPPMAN. (*Shakes hands with* THROTTLEBOTTOM) Sure.

(Together)

(WAITER *enters R. with White Rock, etc. Places them on table by bed, and comes down R. of* LIPPMAN.)

FULTON. What's your name again?

THROTTLEBOTTOM. Alexander—

FULTON. Of course! I nominated you! Alexander! Boys, this is— What's your first name, Mr. Alexander?

THROTTLEBOTTOM. That's my first name. Alexander.

FULTON. Alexander Alexander.

GILHOOLEY. Well, that certainly is a coincidence. (WAITER *taps* LIPPMAN *on arm.* LYONS *up* C. *to table—takes cigar.*)

THROTTLEBOTTOM. But that isn't my last name. It's Throttlebottom.

GILHOOLEY. *(Crossing* L.) Oh, well, that's different.

LIPPMAN. *(As the* WAITER *hands him the check)* Throttle what?

THROTTLEBOTTOM. Bottom.

LIPPMAN. How do you spell it?

THROTTLEBOTTOM. *(As he starts to spell,* LIPPMAN *takes the check from the* WAITER *and writes)* "T-h-r-o-t-t-l-e-b-o-t-t-o-m."

LIPPMAN. Right! And thank you very much. (WAITER *exits* R. *with check, pushed out by* LIPPMAN.)

FULTON. Well, sir, we're very glad, indeed, to see you, and very proud to have you on our ticket. Won't you sit down? (LYONS *puts chair* L. *of table.* ALL *sit, leaving no place for* THROTTLEBOTTOM.)

THROTTLEBOTTOM. *(After a good look around)* Thanks. I won't sit. I'm only going to stay a minute. There's something I came up to see you about.

FULTON. What's that?

THROTTLEBOTTOM. Being Vice-President. I want to know if you won't let me off.

FULTON. *(Rises)* What?   } *(Together)*
GILHOOLEY. *(Rises)* What do you mean?

THROTTLEBOTTOM. I don't want to be Vice-President. I want to resign.

FULTON. Why, you can't do that! (ALL *rise.*)

JONES. *(Rises)* That's treason!

LYONS. Absurd, suh!   } *(Together)*

LIPPMAN. *(Rises)* Why don't you want to be Vice-President? That's a good job.

THROTTLEBOTTOM. It's—it's on account of my mother. Suppose she found out?

FULTON. You've got a mother?

GILHOOLEY. *(To* OTHERS) Boys, he's got a mother. (JONES *and* GILHOOLEY *take off hats.*)

LIPPMAN. This is a fine time to tell us.

FULTON. (L.) Yes, why didn't you tell us? You can't back out now. Everything's printed.

GILHOOLEY. *(Ease* C.) Listen, she'll never hear about it.

JONES. Of course not.

THROTTLEBOTTOM. But maybe she will. Somebody may tell her.

LIPPMAN. Who'll tell her?

FULTON. Why, nobody'll know. (LYONS *pours drink—hands it to* LIPPMAN.)

GILHOOLEY. *(Gets drink from table—eases* R.) You'll forget it yourself in three months. (JONES *eases* R.)

FULTON. Of course.

LIPPMAN. *(Crossing* C. *to* THROTTLEBOTTOM) Besides, suppose something should happen to the President?

THROTTLEBOTTOM. What?

LIPPMAN. Suppose something should happen to the President? Then you become President.

THROTTLEBOTTOM. Me?

LIPPMAN. Sure.

THROTTLEBOTTOM. President! Say!

LIPPMAN. Let's drink to that! *(To* LYONS) Bob! To our next President! (LYONS *passes the glass to* LIPPMAN, *right under* THROTTLEBOTTOM'S *nose, as* THROTTLEBOTTOM *makes a futile pass for it.* JONES *passes a glass to* FULTON.)

GILHOOLEY. Our next President!

JONES. *(By* R. *door)* Our next President!

(WINTERGREEN *enters as this line is being spoken, and simultaneously* THROTTLEBOTTOM, *seeing that there is no glass for him, makes a dash for the bathroom, from which he emerges with a green bathroom glass, a moment later.*)

WINTERGREEN. I'll drink to that! *(Takes the glass in the extended arm of* JONES *and drinks. There is an ad lib. greeting from* ALL. *Hands back glass and crosses* C. *to* THROTTLEBOTTOM.)

LIPPMAN. Well, how's the candidate?

WINTERGREEN. Thirsty. Say, doesn't a fellow get a drink? *(He sees the drink* THROTTLEBOTTOM *has just poured for himself, and takes it from his hand)* Ah! Thank you, waiter. And get me one of those dill pickles, will you?

THROTTLEBOTTOM. But I'm not—

WINTERGREEN. There they are—right over there. (THROTTLEBOTTOM *obediently goes for the pickle* R. *at bed table.)* Well, gentlemen, it certainly was a great convention. I never expected to get the nomination. Didn't *want* the nomination. Never was so surprised as when my name came up. *(Takes pickle from* THROTTLEBOTTOM, *and gives him the empty glass.* THROTTLEBOTTOM *goes back to table and pours another drink.)*

GILHOOLEY. Say, who brought it up, anyhow?

FULTON. Yah. Who was that in the back calling "Wintergreen!"

WINTERGREEN. That was me. Most spontaneous thing you ever saw. So here I am, gentlemen—nominated by the people, absolutely my own master, and ready to do any dirty work the committee suggests. *(In one movement takes the full glass* THROTTLEBOTTOM *has finally succeeded in getting for himself, and replaces it with the pickle he has been holding in his own hand.* THROTTLEBOTTOM *returns pickle to table.)*

LYONS. *Mister* President— (FULTON *drops down* R.C.)

WINTERGREEN. I'll drink to that, too! Anything else, gentlemen? Anything at all! What's the matter, Fulton? Something wrong? You're not sober, are you?

FULTON. *(His tone belying the words)* No, no! I'm all right.

WINTERGREEN. Must be something up. *(A look at the* OTHERS *as he puts down his glass)* What's the matter?

LIPPMAN. *(Deprecatingly)* A lot of schmoos.

FULTON. Well, it's this way. Begins to look as though there may be a little trouble ahead.

WINTERGREEN. Trouble? (THROTTLEBOTTOM *drops* R. *of* FULTON.)

FULTON. I don't think people are quite satisfied with the party record.

WINTERGREEN. Who said they were?

FULTON. Well, you know what Lincoln said.

WINTERGREEN. Who?

FULTON. Lincoln.

GILHOOLEY. What did he say?

WINTERGREEN. Was it funny?

FULTON. "You can fool some of the people all the time, and you can fool all of the people some of the time, but you can't fool all of the people all of the time."

THROTTLEBOTTOM. *(His lips start moving as* FULTON *speaks, and at the last half of the speech he is unable to keep silent, so with great assurance he comes in on)* "—but you can't fool all of the people some— *(Corrects himself)* —all of the time."

WINTERGREEN. Was that Lincoln?

THROTTLEBOTTOM. Abraham J. Lincoln.

WINTERGREEN. It's different nowadays. People are bigger suckers.

GILHOOLEY. *(Drops down* L.C.) Yes, but we made one bad mistake. Never should have sold Rhode Island.

WINTERGREEN. *(Crossing to* GILHOOLEY) Rhode Island?

Nobody missed it! *(A gesture indicating its size)* H'm. Where is Rhode Island now? Anybody know?

THROTTLEBOTTOM. It's in Providence.

FULTON. Wall Street, some place. Never get it back.

WINTERGREEN. *(Crossing* C. *to* FULTON. *A slap of the hands)* I'll tell you what! We'll leave it out of the campaign— not mention it! *(There is a chorus of approval.* JONES: *"Say, that might do it!"* LYONS: *"That's great, suh!"* LIPPMAN: *"Sure it would!"* GILHOOLEY: *"That's the idea!"* FULTON: *"Swell.")* Yes, sir, that's the idea—we won't mention it!

THROTTLEBOTTOM. But suppose somebody else brings it up?

WINTERGREEN. Don't answer 'em! It takes two to make an argument. *(Notices, but does not recognize* THROTTLEBOTTOM. *Crosses to* FULTON. THROTTLEBOTTOM *backs away.)* I thought this was a closed meeting.

FULTON. Sure it is. Why?

WINTERGREEN. *(Gesturing and whispering)* Who's that?

FULTON. *(Also whispering)* Vice-President.

WINTERGREEN. *(Whispers)* What? *(Shrugs his shoulders.)*

FULTON. Oh—this is Mr. Wintergreen. Mr.—ah—ah—

THROTTLEBOTTOM. *(Taking a moment to remember)* Ah— ah—Throttlebottom. *(They shake hands—an exchange of "How do you do's.")*

WINTERGREEN. Haven't I seen you before some place?

THROTTLEBOTTOM. I gave you that dill pickle.

WINTERGREEN. *(Eases down* C.) Of course. (THROTTLE- BOTTOM *crosses* R.)

FULTON. But, look here, Mr. President—it's not only Rhode Island. There've been a whole lot of things the last four years.

GILHOOLEY. How about the four years before that?

WINTERGREEN. *(Up* C. *to* JONES) I'll tell you what—let's stick to the party record of Seventeen Hundred and Seventy-Six. That was a good year.

LIPPMAN. What's the matter with Fourteen Ninety-Two?

WINTERGREEN. We can use that year, too. We won't men- tion anything before Fourteen Nineteen-Two, or after Seven- teen Seventy-Six. That gives us pretty nearly three hundred years.

FULTON. Say, that's great!,

LYONS. *(Rises, drops* L. *of* WINTERGREEN*)* But, just a min- ute, suh! Down South the people want to hear about the Civil War.

WINTERGREEN. What year was that?

LYONS. *(Searching pocket)* Well, I haven't got the exact figures with me, but it was around Eighteen Hundred and Twelve.

THROTTLEBOTTOM. What year was Eighteen Twelve?

WINTERGREEN. Well, how about putting the Civil War back to Seventeen Seventy-Six? I think it's safer.

LYONS. Perfectly satisfactory, suh. Perfectly satisfactory. $\Big\}$ *(Together)*

JONES. Eminently fair.

FULTON. Yah, but it isn't enough.

GILHOOLEY. *(Dropping down* C., *then* L.*)* No! What we need is a good live issue!

FULTON. *(Eases* R. LYONS *crosses down* L.; *pulls chair down a little and sits)* Yes! That's what we need—an issue. Something that everybody is interested in, and that doesn't matter a damn. Something the party can stand on. (LIPPMAN *sits* L. *of table.)*

THROTTLEBOTTOM. Excuse me, gentlemen, but what party are we?

WINTERGREEN. We've got plenty of time for that. The important thing is to get elected.

JONES. You see, we're Republicans in most states.

LYONS. *(Rises)* But the South is Democratic. *(Sits.)*

JONES. Oh, sure. We're Democrats down there.

THROTTLEBOTTOM. *(To* WINTERGREEN*)* I had a dog that was bitten by a Democrat.

WINTERGREEN. *(Whispers to* JONES*)* Who is that?

JONES. *(Whispers)* Vice-President. *(The* CHAMBERMAID *enters* R.*)*

CHAMBERMAID. Excuse me. *(Crosses back of group and exits into bathroom* L.*)*

FULTON. Boys, I tell you this is serious. We've got to get something that'll take hold of the popular imagination—sweep the country.

LIPPMAN. *(Dropping down* L.C.*)* The country could stand a good sweeping.

JONES. Mr. Fulton is quite correct.

CHAMBERMAID. *(Re-enters from bathroom. Crossing* R. *between* GILHOOLEY *and* JONES *to* L. *of* THROTTLEBOTTOM*)* Can I turn the bed down now?

FULTON. What?

CHAMBERMAID. Can I turn the bed down now?

FULTON. Say—come here a minute. *(The* MAID *and* THROTTLEBOTTOM *both start toward* FULTON. *To* THROTTLEBOTTOM*)* No, not you. *(To* CHAMBERMAID*)* You're an American citizen?

CHAMBERMAID. Yes, sir.

FULTON. Ever vote?

CHAMBERMAID. Oh, *no*, sir.

FULTON. What do you care more about than anything else in the world?

CHAMBERMAID. I don't know. Money, I guess.

GILHOOLEY. That's no good.

WINTERGREEN. It brings up Rhode Island.

JONES. That's right.

CHAMBERMAID. *(Looking at* THROTTLEBOTTOM*)* What?

THROTTLEBOTTOM. I didn't say anything—

FULTON. Of course, money. We all want money. But there must be something else, isn't there?

CHAMBERMAID. *(Thinks)* No—I like money.

FULTON. But after money, what?

CHAMBERMAID. Well, maybe love.

FULTON. Love?

CHAMBERMAID. Yeh. You know, to meet a nice young fellow that's crazy about you, and you're crazy about him, and you get engaged, and then you get married, and—*you* know—*(To* THROTTLEBOTTOM*)* —love.

THROTTLEBOTTOM. Sure.

FULTON. Oh, yes, all right. Thank you. Thank you very much.

CHAMBERMAID. Shall I turn the bed down now, sir?

FULTON. Not now. Come back later on.

CHAMBERMAID. Yes, sir. *(Starts to go.)*

FULTON. Ah—here you are. *(Gives her a coin.* THROTTLEBOTTOM *reaches for it.)* No, not you.

CHAMBERMAID. Thank you, sir. *(Exits* R. JONES *up to table.)*

LIPPMAN. Well, you got a lot out of that.

WINTERGREEN. Put women into politics and that's what you get. Love.

GILHOOLEY. Love!

FULTON. What's the matter with love?

WINTERGREEN. *(Disgustedly)* A-ah!

THROTTLEBOTTOM. I like love!

FULTON. People *do* care more about love than anything else. Why, they steal for it; they even kill for it.

WINTERGREEN. *(Up* C. *and back)* But will they vote for it?

FULTON. You bet they will! If we could find some way to put it over—why, we could get every vote in the country! Everybody loves a lover; the whole world loves a— *(Stops as he gets an idea; looks fixedly at* WINTERGREEN.*)*

WINTERGREEN. *(Down* C.*)* What's the matter?

FULTON. I've got it!

THROTTLEBOTTOM. *(To* OTHERS*)* He's got it.

WINTERGREEN. Got what?

FULTON. You've got to fall in love!

WINTERGREEN. You're crazy!

FULTON. (LYONS *rises and crosses* L.C.*)* You've got to fall in love with a typical American girl.

WINTERGREEN. Huh?

LIPPMAN. What good's that? *(Together)*

GILHOOLEY. What are you talking about?

JONES. What for?

FULTON. Wait a minute! You make love to her from now till Election Day as no girl was ever made love to before.

WINTERGREEN. What's the gag?

GILHOOLEY. Yah! *(Together)*

LIPPMAN. So what?

FULTON. *(Crossing to* WINTERGREEN*)* My God, are you blind? You do this right and you'll get elected by the greatest majority that the American people ever gave a candidate! You'll get every vote!

WINTERGREEN. But wait a minute—

GILHOOLEY. I think there's something in it.

JONES. It sounds good.

LYONS. Certainly does! *(Together)*

LIPPMAN. Say!

FULTON. I tell you it's great!

WINTERGREEN. But just a minute—

FULTON. You'll go down in history as the greatest lover this country has ever known! You'll be the romantic ideal of every man, woman and child in America!

(WARN Blackout.)

WINTERGREEN. Oh, no! I don't want anything like that!

FULTON. But, man, it's the biggest thing in the world! A hundred million hearts will beat as one; they'll follow your courtship in every State in the Union! You meet the girl, you fall in love with her, you propose, you're accepted, and you're swept into the White House on a tidal wave of love!

WINTERGREEN. But there's nobody I'm in love with! I'm not in love with anybody!

FULTON. We'll get a girl. That'll be easy.

LIPPMAN. My wife's sister!

FULTON. I've got the idea! We'll have a contest—a nationwide contest to select Miss White House—choose the most beautiful girl from every State—get them all together at Atlantic City, pick the winner, and you fall in love with her!

WINTERGREEN. But suppose I *don't* fall in love with her?

THROTTLEBOTTOM. Then *I* get her! (ALL *to table for drinks except* FULTON.)

FULTON. *(Goes to phone)* You can't *help* falling in love with her! The most beautiful girl in America! I tell you this is wonderful! *(Into the telephone)* Give me Beekman five thousand.

WINTERGREEN. *(Through* FULTON's *phone conversation)* Give me another drink!

LIPPMAN. Let's all have another drink! Scotch or rye, Jack?

WINTERGREEN. Both!

FULTON. *(At phone)* Give me Jenkins! Hello!

LIPPMAN. *(With bottle)* Say when!

FULTON. That's what I said—Jenkins!

WINTERGREEN. *(Stopping* LIPPMAN; *there is hardly anything in the glass)* That's enough! *(Takes the bottle instead of the glass.)*

FULTON. Jenkins? Fulton! Stop the presses! John P. Wintergreen will run for President on a one-word platform: "Love!" National beauty contest in Atlantic City to select Miss White House! Now, listen! I want a love cartoon on the front page of every one of my papers from now till Election Day! Right! And call up Al Smith and tell him I want a thousand words on love tomorrow morning!

BLACKOUT.

ACT ONE

SCENE III

End of second bar of introduction LIGHTS on.

SCENE: *A drop in One.*

The boardwalk in Atlantic City.

AT RISE: DIANA *enters Left, followed by* 12 GIRLS. *At the same time* 12 *more* GIRLS *enter* R. *They parade on, in showgirl fashion, singing.* ALL *are in bathing suits.*

GIRLS.
Who is the lucky girl to be?
Ruler of Washington, D. C.?
Who is to be the blushing bride?

Who will sleep at the President's side?
Strike up the cymbals, drum and fife!
One of us is the President's future wife!

8 GIRLS.
We're in Atlantic City
To meet with the committee,

8 OTHERS.
And when they've made their mind up
The winner will be signed up.

8 SHOWGIRLS.
The prize is consequential—
Presidential!
Our bodies will bear witness
To our fitness.

ALL.
If a girl is sexy
She may be Mrs. Prexy!
One of us is the President's future wife!

(The two melodies are repeated together, the SHOWGIRLS *singing the first verse, the* DANCERS *the other. At its conclusion, the* PHOTOGRAPHERS, *led by* JENKINS, *enter* R. *First* 4 GIRLS *kneel. Second line lean over.* DIANA *and* JENKINS *are* C.)

PHOTOGRAPHERS.
More important than a photograph of Parliament,
Or a shipwreck on the sea—
What'll raise the circulation
Of our paper through the nation
Is the dimple on your knee.

(WARN Blackout.)
More important than a photograph of Parliament
Or a Western spelling bee,
Or the latest thing in science,
For our pleasure loving clients
Is the dimple on your knee.

(SHOWGIRLS *exit* L.)

What our readers love to see
Is the dimple on your knee,
What our readers love to see
Is the dimple on your knee.

(A PHOTOGRAPHER *kneeling between each* 2 GIRLS.)

GIRLS.
More important than a photograph of Parliament
Is the dimple on my knee.
But supposing I am losing
When the judges are a-choosing—
What will my poor future be?

Do I have to go back to the cafeteria
With my lovely dimpled knee?
Does a girl who's so ambitious
Have to work at washing dishes?
I'm afraid that worries me.

PHOTOGRAPHERS. *(Rise)*
Don't worry, little girl,
For even if you lose the prize—
Don't worry, little girl,
Myself, I can't resist your eyes.

GIRLS.
I'll worry, little boy,
Until you tell what's on your mind.

(The GIRLS *cross to* R.; *the* BOYS *to* L. DIANA *exits* R.*)*

PHOTOGRAPHERS.
Don't worry, little girl,
I've asked my heart and this is what I find—
Don't worry, little girl;
Don't worry, little girl.

GIRLS.
Why shouldn't we worry?

PHOTOGRAPHERS.
Because, because, because, because,
Because you're in the money
With a smile that's sweet and sunny—
I could fall for you myself.
Because, because, because, because
Your looks are so appealing
They have given me a feeling,
I could fall for you myself.

*(*GIRLS *move* L.*)*

The thrills you're sending through me
Are doing something to me!
The opposite of gloomy—
If *they* don't want you, *I* want you!

(4 BOYS *cross* R. GIRLS L.)

Because, because, because, because,
Because your ways are simple,
And your knee can show a dimple,
I could fall for you myself.

(First dance chorus—4 PHOTOGRAPHERS R. *and* L. GIRLS C. JENKINS *and* GIRLS *dance one chorus.* JENKINS *dances,* GIRLS *gesture,* PHOTOGRAPHERS *sing one chorus.* PHOTOGRAPHERS *exit* R. *and* L. *at end of chorus. Last* 16 *bars* GIRLS C. JENKINS *and* GIRLS *exit*—32 *bars.)*

BLACKOUT.

ACT ONE

SCENE IV

When drop is up stage and arc LIGHTS on.

SCENE: *Parlor of an Atlantic City hotel suite. Large double doors* R. *and* L. *A balcony up* C., *elevated three steps. Curved backless settees* R.C. *and* L.C., *two chairs against the back wall* R. *and* L. *of the arch leading to the balcony. A small table down* R. *and a desk against the* L. *wall, above the large doors.*

AT RISE: 8 GIRLS *in bathing suits are on stage.* MARY TURNER, *distinguished from the others by the fact that she wears a dress, is seated at the desk. From the moment of the rise,* OTHER GIRLS *in bathing suits stream on from the entrance at Left, to make a total of twenty-four.*

As the LIGHTS come on, FULTON *and* GILHOOLEY *enter* R., *followed by* 4 MEN *with movie cameras, which are set up down* R.

GILHOOLEY. *(To* MOVIEMEN*)* Come on, boys! Set 'em up right here—that'll give you a good angle! Hello, ladies!
FULTON. *(Enters* R.; *crosses* L. *Speaking through* GILHOOLEY'S *speech)* Well, well! What a crowd! How are you,

ladies? This certainly is a big day, all right! Must be ten thousand people outside this hotel! Never saw so much excitement in all my life!

GIRL. (R.C.) Say! What does a President's wife have to do, anyhow?

GILHOOLEY. *(Over R., ease up and over L.)* That depends on the President.

MARY. *(Coming downstage to FULTON)* Good morning, Mr. Fulton.

FULTON. *(Both L.C.)* Well, Miss Turner! Having quite a day, huh?

MARY. Quite a day, Mr. Fulton.

FULTON. Heard some very nice things about the way you've been handling this. Afraid I'll have to give you a raise.

MARY. Well, I'm afraid I'll have to take it. *(Goes to desk, then exits L. LYONS and JONES enter R.)*

LYONS. Afternoon, gentlemen! Ladies!

FULTON. Ah, here's some of the committee now! Good afternoon, gentlemen! *(Together)*

JONES. Mr. Fulton! Good afternoon, ladies! Good afternoon! Well! Quite a battery you have here—quite a battery!

LYONS. Gentlemen of the press!

JONES. Very glad to see you, gentlemen. Always glad to meet the newspaper boys. *(JENKINS enters R., followed by 2 BOYS.)*

JENKINS. *(To FULTON, who is L.C.)* Good morning, Chief!

FULTON. Oh, hello, Jenkins!

JONES. (R.C.) Hello, there! I've met you before. Never forget a face! Just tell me—we've met before? Am I right?

JENKINS. Right you are, Senator!

JONES. Right! Where was it?

JENKINS. San Francisco. That opium joint on Fourth Street.

JONES. Well, I guess I got the wrong man. Remarkable resemblance, though; remarkable resemblance. *(The GIRLS have laughed at JONES' discomfiture.)*

THROTTLEBOTTOM. *(Enters R. Crossing C.)* Hello, everybody! Hello, Mr. Fulton!

GILHOOLEY. Hello, there!

JONES. How are you? *(Together)*

LYONS. Good morning, suh!

FULTON. Who is that guy?

GILHOOLEY. Vice-President.

FULTON. Oh, yes. Hello! How are you?

THROTTLEBOTTOM. Are these the girls? I'm Mr. Throttle-bottom. *(To a* GIRL*)* Hello! How are you?

GIRL. *(Just* L. *of* C.*)* Fine!

THROTTLEBOTTOM. Is your mother down here with you?

GIRL. Yes, sir.

THROTTLEBOTTOM. Oh! Well! Never mind! *(He turns to another* GIRL *on his* R.*)*

FULTON. *(Goes to* THROTTLEBOTTOM*)* Say, look here a minute. You know, Vice-Presidents don't usually go around in public. They're not supposed to be seen.

THROTTLEBOTTOM. But I'm not Vice-President yet. Couldn't I go around a little longer?

GILHOOLEY. That isn't the point. If you're going to be Vice-President you've got to practice up for it. You've got to go in hiding.

THROTTLEBOTTOM. But I came up the back way.

FULTON. You shouldn't have come at all. Suppose somebody sees you?

GILHOOLEY. We'd lose the election.

THROTTLEBOTTOM. You mean you want me to hide from everybody?

JONES. That's it! } *(Together)*
FULTON. Right! }

THROTTLEBOTTOM. I could go back to my old business.

FULTON. What's that?

THROTTLEBOTTOM. I used to be a hermit.

FULTON. Great! } *(Together)*
GILHOOLEY. That's the idea! }

THROTTLEBOTTOM. But I thought you might want me to make some speeches.

FULTON. No, no!

GILHOOLEY. You just go and sit in your cave.

THROTTLEBOTTOM. Well—I could go back to the cave and write my speeches there.

FULTON. That's the idea! (THROTTLEBOTTOM *starts* R. COMMITTEE *eases* R. *after him.* LYONS *stays* C.*)*

JONES. *(Crossing around back to up* L.*)* Perfect!

GILHOOLEY. And make 'em there, too!

(Together)

JONES. Don't let anybody find you—don't let anybody see you.

THROTTLEBOTTOM. I won't—I won't even come out in February to cast my shadow. *(Exits* R. GILHOOLEY *goes up* R.C.*)*

DIANA. *(Enters* L. *Dropping down* C.*)* Mo'nin', Senator Lyons.

LYONS. *(C.)* Well, Miss Devereaux! And how is the fairest flower of the South?

DIANA. *(Thick Southern accent)* Senator Lyons, that's the prettiest thing been said to me since I left Louisiana. I sure been gettin' pow'ful homesick.

GIRL. She sure is getting pow'ful Southern.

LYONS. You're just a breath of the old Southland.

DIANA. You keep on sayin' sweet things like that and I'm just going to throw my arms right around your neck.

FULTON. You never made me an offer like that, Miss Devereaux.

DIANA. Why, Mr. Fulton!

FULTON. Yes, sir; when I look around I'm sorry I didn't run for President myself.

DIANA. You'd make a mighty fine consolation prize. Wouldn't he, girls? *(The GIRLS assent.)*

FULTON. Now, now! Matter of fact, we're getting up some consolation prizes. Got that list, Jenkins?

JENKINS. *(Crossing to FULTON—then R.C. to GIRLS)* Here you are, sir.

FULTON. *(Down R.C.)* Of course, the first prize, as you all know, is Mr. Wintergreen himself. The second prize is a season pass to Coney Island. And the third prize is an autographed photograph of Clara Bow, or ten cents in gold. *(A murmur of excitement from the GIRLS. Enter R., WINTERGREEN and LIPPMAN. There is a buzz at their entrance.)* Well, well! The candidate himself! Hello, Jack!

WINTERGREEN. Hello, there!

FULTON. *(LIPPMAN drops down R.)* Ladies, permit me to introduce your future husband, John P. Wintergreen! *(The GIRLS greet him.)* Here they are, Jack. How do you like 'em? *(Down R.)*

WINTERGREEN. Why, they're wonderful. Hello. *(Crossing up C. The GIRLS respond.)* How are you? *(Another response. Having done his duty, he crosses back to FULTON.)*

FULTON. Say something to them.

WINTERGREEN. *(Going up C.)* Well, ladies, this certainly is a pleasure. All I can say is I love you, and you are the only girls I have ever loved. (GILHOOLEY, *who is standing in the line with the GIRLS, giggles.)* Say, you're not one of them, are you? (GILHOOLEY, *affronted, moves out of line.)* And after we're married, I hope you'll all be happy, and— *(Back to FULTON, R.C.)* Listen, Fulton, I can't go through with this.

FULTON. You've got to go through with it.

WINTERGREEN. But I don't know any of these girls! How can I marry them? If it was only somebody I knew, like—

(Crossing R.*)* Lippman—whatever became of your wife's sister?

LIPPMAN. *(Down* R., *with a shake of the head)* Not in a bathing suit.

FULTON. By the way, I want you to meet Miss Diana Devereaux.

LYONS. Miss Devereaux, may I have the honor—

DIANA. *(Cutting through his speech as she crosses to him)* Mr. President, I'm mighty happy to meet you! I hope we're going to see a lot of each other.

WINTERGREEN. Any hope of yours, Miss Devereaux, is a hope of mine—I hope.

DIANA. You keep on saying sweet things like that and I'm just going to throw my arms right around your neck. *(The remaining* TWENTY-THREE GIRLS *chime in when she is halfway through the sentence and finish it with her, Southern accent and all.)*

WINTERGREEN. Seems to be quite an echo here.

DIANA. *(Playing with his lapel)* Mr. Wintergreen—have you-all got a fraternity pin?

WINTERGREEN. Well, would a safety pin do?

DIANA. Mr. Wintergreen, you've got the grandest sense of humor. *(Still working the lapel.* MARY *re-enters* L.*)* Oh—Mr. Wintergreen—

MARY. All right, Mr. Fulton. *(Goes to desk.)*

FULTON. *(Down* R.*)* And now, ladies—attention, please! The time has come for the final test. *(The* GIRLS *start a general primping and there is an excited buzz.)* It has been a gruelling contest—you have been under a great strain. And we of the committee want to thank you—and through you the three million others who took part in this contest, only ninety-eight percent of whom had to be sent home for misbehavior. *(Crosses to* C.*)* And, now, ladies, the judges await you. And may the best girl win. (COMMITTEE *forms up* C. *MUSIC.)*

GIRLS.
    Who is the lucky girl to be—
    Ruler of Washington, D. C.?

DIANA. *(Pulling* WINTERGREEN *to* C.*)*
    Bye-bye, Mr. President—I'm a-prayin'
    I'm the little lady they're okayin'.

(DIANA *starts* L.)

GIRLS. *(Exiting* L., *followed by* DIANA)
    Strike up the cymbals, drum and fife!
    One of us is the President's future wife!

COMMITTEE.
  We'll get you, Mrs. Wintergreen.
WINTERGREEN.
  Oh-o-o-o-o-o-o.
COMMITTEE.
  We'll get you, Mrs. Wintergreen.
WINTERGREEN.
  Oh-o-o-o-o-o-o-o-o-o.
COMMITTEE. *(Down stage 4 steps, back 4 steps)*
  We'll present you with a bride!
  She will be the Nation's pride!
  Ta-Ta-Ta-Ta-Ta-Ta.

(They exit L. *on musical ending.* WINTERGREEN *is left on stage with* MARY. WINTERGREEN, *calling "good-bye," watches them exit. Looks after them thoughtfully a moment, then starts to pace up and down. He pulls out handkerchief and mops his brow.* MARY *takes papers from desk, starts toward balcony.)*

WINTERGREEN. *(As he sees her)* Oh! Say! *(She stops.)* You haven't got a drink on you, have you?
  MARY. Why, no. I'm sorry.
  WINTERGREEN. Oh, that's all right. Didn't want it anyhow. *(Crossing down* C. *Pacing.)*
  MARY. *(Dropping down* L.C.*)* Little bit nervous?
  WINTERGREEN. *(Whirling)* Who? Me? What have I got to be nervous about?
  MARY. That's what I was wondering. Twenty-four of the most beautiful girls in the country—and you get the winner. Lots of men would like to be in your shoes.
  WINTERGREEN. *(Crossing to her)* Yeah, but it's my bedroom slippers I'm worrying about. Say, you've been watching them—who do you think it's going to be?
  MARY. Oh, I couldn't say. Likely to be any one of them.
  WINTERGREEN. That's what I was afraid of. Which one? What's your guess?
  MARY. *(Sits settee* L.*)* Well, don't hold me to it, but I shouldn't be surprised if it were Miss Devereaux.
  WINTERGREEN. *(Up to her by* L. *end of settee)* Devereaux! I thought so! Is that the—ah—the one with the Southern exposure? *(Indicating the figure.)*
  MARY. That's Miss Devereaux. She's a good-looking girl, don't you think?
  WINTERGREEN. *(Doubtfully)* Yes, she's a good-looking girl, all right.

MARY. *(In broad Southern accent)* Don't you-all like good-looking girls?

WINTERGREEN. *(Leans R. of settee)* Down Carolina way we're all a-crazy about good-looking girls. But we-all don't like 'em talking that-a-way.

MARY. How do you-all like 'em to talk, sure enough?

WINTERGREEN. We-all like them-all to let us-all do the talk-ing. *(Abandons the dialect)* Say, that's terrible, isn't it? *(Eases C.)* If she wins would I have to listen to that all the time? *(Back to her.)*

MARY. But she does it charmingly. And she's very beauti-ful.

WINTERGREEN. Beautiful, yeah—I like a beautiful girl—they're all right—*(He stumbles)*—but when a fellow gets mar-ried he wants a home, a mother for his children.

MARY. *(Rises and drops down L.C.)* You've got children?

WINTERGREEN. *(Down to her)* No, no; I mean if I was married. You see, when you're married—well, *you* know.

MARY. Well, I think Miss Devereaux might listen to rea-son. And she'd make a very beautiful mother for your chil-dren.

WINTERGREEN. Beautiful! I don't know anything about these girls—whether they can sew, or make a bed, or cook. They don't look as though they'd ever had a skillet in their hands. Say, what *is* a skillet?

MARY. You wouldn't have to worry about that in the White House. They have plenty of servants there.

WINTERGREEN. Yeah, but some day we'll have to move out of the White House. Then what? The Old Presidents' Home? There'll be no servants there. She'll *have* to cook; then what?

MARY. *(Eases L.)* Then she'll cook. And like it.

WINTERGREEN. *(After her)* But will *I* like it? Why, the average girl today can't cook—she can't even broil an egg. *(Crossing R.)*

MARY. Nonsense! Every girl can cook.

WINTERGREEN. *(Scornfully)* Every girl can cook—can *you?* *(Stops R.C.)*

MARY. I certainly can.

WINTERGREEN. Then what are you doing here?

MARY. *(Right back at him)* I'm holding down a job! *(Crossing R. to him)* And I can cook, and sew, and make lace curtains, and bake the best darned corn muffins you ever ate. And what do you know about that?

WINTERGREEN. Corn muffins? Did **you say corn muffins?**
MARY. **Yes, corn muffins!**

WINTERGREEN. Corn muffins! You haven't got one on you, have you?

MARY. *(Crossing him* R.*)* I haven't far to go.

WINTERGREEN. I'm crazy about corn muffins. I eat them all the time.

MARY. *(Gets lunch box from table down* R.*)* It's lunch, but you can have it. *(Back to him.)*

WINTERGREEN. Oh, I couldn't do that! *(He fumbles in box, looking at her.)*

MARY. Please! The second from the left is a corn muffin. That's an apple.

WINTERGREEN. Oh, that's an apple. *(Picking up a muffin)* Well! You must let me take *you* to lunch some day. Mmm! Delicious! *(Samples it)* Why—it melts in the mouth!

MARY. *(Putting the box back on table* R.*)* And I'm the only person in the world who can make them without corn.

WINTERGREEN. Without—say, do you know I don't even know your name.

MARY. *(Back to him)* That's right—you don't.

WINTERGREEN. Mine's Wintergreen.

MARY. *I* know. Mine's Turner.

WINTERGREEN. Just Turner?

MARY. Mary Turner.

WINTERGREEN. *(Suddenly)* Say, why in God's name didn't you get into this contest?

MARY. *(Crossing him* L.*)* One of the three million?

WINTERGREEN. Well, you know what the first prize is? *(Eases* R. *and back.)*

MARY. Yeah, can you imagine?

WINTERGREEN. And you get your picture in the paper.

MARY. Having tea on the lawn with the Filipino delegation. And you throwing the medicine ball at the cabinet.

WINTERGREEN. Oh, do we have to have a cabinet?

MARY. What would you throw the medicine ball at? Me?

WINTERGREEN. *(Suddenly sobered)* Gosh, it'd be fun with you. We could have a grand time.

MARY. *(The Southern accent)* Why, Mr. Wintergreen—

WINTERGREEN. No, I mean it. *(NOISE off* L.*)* Listen—I've only got a minute—maybe less than that! I love you! I know it's awful sudden, but in a minute it'll be too late! Let's elope—let's get out of here! *(Pulls her* R.*)*

MARY. But—but wait a minute. You don't know me. *(Pulls him back.)*

WINTERGREEN. I know you better than those girls! *(A gesture)* You can make corn muffins, and—you're darned cute-looking, and—I love you! *(Pulls her* R.*)*

MARY. But I don't know *you! (Stops him.)*

WINTERGREEN. What's there to know? I'm young, I'm a swell conversationalist, and I've got a chance to be President! And, besides that—you love me!

MARY. But it's absurd. Why, you can't—

WINTERGREEN. The hell I can't! *(He seizes her and starts kissing her)* It's fate, Mary, that's what it is—fate! *(Kisses her again)* Why, we were meant for each other—you and me!

MARY. You and *I!*

WINTERGREEN. All right, you and I! *(Continues kissing her.)*

(The sound of TALKING off. MARY and WINTERGREEN go down R. The committee—FULTON, GILHOOLEY, LYONS, LIPPMAN and JONES—enter L.; come to C.)

FULTON.
    As the chairman of the committee
    I announce we've made our choice;
    Ev'ry lover from Dubuque to Jersey City
    Should rejoice!

COMMITTEE.
    We rejoice.

(8 CONTEST JUDGES, in cutaways, enter L. to above the settees, singing)

JUDGES *and* COMMITTEE.
    When the angels up there designed her,
    They designed a thoroughbred;
    And on March the Fourth the President will find her
    Worthy of his board and bed.

(MUSIC changes to waltz, FULTON speaking through it.)

FULTON. (C.) And now it thrills me to introduce the rarest of American beauties, the future first lady of the land—a fit consort for the ruler of our country—gentlemen—Miss Diana Devereaux! *(Crosses L. to escort DIANA down C.)*

(DIANA appears L. with a golden crown on her head, followed by all the other GIRLS, still in bathing suits. ALL sing as she parades to C., close to where WINTERGREEN and MARY are standing.)

ALL. *(As DIANA makes circle of COMMITTEE—then up C.)*
    How beautiful, beautiful, beautiful,
    How utterly, utterly so!

The charming, the gracious, the dutiful
Diana Devereaux.

FULTON. *(Spoken)* The committee will now tell why she was chosen—with music!

ALL.
Never was there a girl so fair!
Never was there a form so rare!

DIANA. *(Spoken)* Ah could throw mah arms right around your neck!

ALL.
A voice so lyrical
Is given few;
Her eyes a miracle
Of Prussian blue;
Ruby lips and a foot so small;
As for hips—she has none at all!

(LYONS *moves back.*)

GILHOOLEY. (R. *of* DIANA)
Did you ever see such footsies,
Or a more enticing limb?

LIPPMAN. (L. *of* DIANA)
And the ankles of her tootsies
Are so slim!

LYONS *and* JUDGES.
What a charming epiglottis!
What a lovely coat of tan!
Oh, the man who isn't hot is
Not a man!

ALL.
She's a bargain to whom she's wed;
More than worthy his board and bed!

FULTON. *(Down L.)*
Says the chairman of the committee,
Let the newsmen now come in.
(*Crosses* C. *to* DIANA. JONES *and* LYONS *down* L.)
For the sound reels you must look your best, my pretty.
Have the interviews begin!

GILHOOLEY *and* LYONS. *(Starting* R.*)*
We shall go and bring them in!

WINTERGREEN. *(Crosses to* C.*)*
Stop! No!
Though this may be a blow
I simply cannot marry
Diana Devereaux!

ALL. *(Two steps forward)*
  What's this? What's this?
  He says he cannot marry
    Diana Devereaux!
COMMITTEE *and* JUDGES.
  You mean you will not marry
    Diana Devereaux!
WINTERGREEN. *(C.)*
  Please understand—it isn't that I would jilt or spurn 'er:
  It's just that I love someone else—
ALL.
  Who?
WINTERGREEN. *(Correcting them)*
  Whom! *(Crosses to* MARY*)*
  Mary Turner.
ALL.
  The man is mad!
  Or else a cad!
  He'll have to take her—
  He can't forsake her!
DIANA. *(Crossing to him)*
  This jilting me,
  It cannot be!
  (Crossing L.*)*
  This lousy action
  Calls for retraction!
COMMITTEE *and* JUDGES.
  We must know why
  You should prefer
  (Pointing to DIANA*)*
  Instead of Di
  (Pointing to MARY*)*
  A girl like her.
GIRLS. *(Same gestures)*
  Yes, tell us why
  You should prefer
  Instead of Di
  A girl like her.
WINTERGREEN. *(Turns to her)*
  All that I can say of Mary Turner
  Is that I love Mary Turner.
COMMITTEE *and* JUDGES.
  What's to be done?
  Though she has won,
  (Indicating DIANA*)*
  Though she is signed up,

He's made his mind up!
His love he'd ruther
(Indicating MARY)
Give to the other.
What shall we do now?
What is our cue now?
DIANA. *(To* COMMITTEE)
He will do nothing of the sort.
First we'll settle this thing in court.
(To WINTERGREEN)
You seem to think Miss Turner hits the spot;
But what has she got that I haven't got?
ALL.
Yes, what has *she* got that *she* hasn't got!
WINTERGREEN. *(To* DIANA)
My Mary makes corn muffins—
Can *you* make corn muffins?
DIANA.
I can't make corn muffins!
ALL. *(Sorrowfully)*
She can't make corn muffins!
WINTERGREEN. *(Takes stage* C.)
Some girls can bake a pie
Made up of prunes and quinces;
Some make an oyster fry—
Others are good at blintzes.
(Crossing R. *to table)*
Some lovely girls have done
Wonders with turkey stuffin's,
(Gets muffins; passes them around. Down R.)
But I have found the one
Who can really make corn muffins.
DIANA. *(Crossing* L.)
Who cares about corn muffins?
All I demand is justice!
(Crossing R.)   *(WARN Draw Curtain.)*

(WINTERGREEN *repeats his verse,* MARY, DANCERS *joining in,
the* COMMITTE, JUDGES *singing an obligato, while* DIANA
and the SHOWGIRLS *sing another counter-melody.)*

COMMITTEE *and* JUDGES.
Corn muffins—
Though other girls are good at turkey stuffin's
She takes the cake—for she can bake—corn muffins,
   Corn muffins—
He's not to blame for falling if she's able

To serve them at his table.
(COMMITTEE *samples muffins.* WINTERGREEN *crosses* L. *with box.)*
They should be happy night and day;
They'll make a couple so delightful;
When two agree on corn muffins
Their marriage is only rightful.

DIANA *and* SHOWGIRLS. *(Simultaneously, to the* COMMITTEE)
Don't surrender!
Don't be tender!
I'm (she's) the winner!
She is a little sinner!
Come! Make your mind up.
I (she) not she—am (is) the one who's really signed up!
(DIANA *starts* R.*)*

ALL.
Great, great!
It really must be fate!

COMMITTEE *and* JUDGES.
We must declare these muffins
The best we ever ate!

GIRLS. *(Singing with* COMMITTEE*)*
There's none but Mary Turner
Could ever be his mate!
(DIANA *exits* R.*)*

BOYS. *(Singing with* COMMITTEE *and* GIRLS)
She can make corn muffins!
She can make corn muffins!

(These couplets are repeated eight times, then ALL *form a picture for the last line)*

ALL.
Let's all rejoice!

DRAW CURTAIN

(ARC LIGHTS OUT)

ACT ONE

SCENE V

Open Drapes.

SCENE: *In one, outside Madison Square Garden.*
In the Centre of the drop are double doors leading into

*the Garden, and through them is seen the corridor. Above
the entrance is a large banner bearing pictures of* WIN-
TERGREEN *and* MARY, *and the inscriptions,* "WOO WITH
WINTERGREEN" *and* "LOVERS! VOTE FOR JOHN AND
MARY."

AT RISE: BAND *enters* L., *followed by* EIGHT MEN (DANCERS).
*They play one chorus of "WINTERGREEN FOR
PRESIDENT," and then a chorus of "LOVE IS SWEEP-
ING THE COUNTRY," on which* JENKINS *and* MISS
BENSON *enter* L.

(JENKINS *and* BENSON *sing Verse and Chorus of "Love Is
Sweeping the Country," at conclusion of which* BAND
exits.)

JENKINS *and* BENSON.
  Why are people gay
  All the night and day,
  Feeling as they never felt before?
BENSON.
  What is this thing
JENKINS.
  That makes them sing?
  Rich man, poor man, thief,
  Doctor, lawyer, chief—
JENKINS *and* BENSON.
  Feel a feeling that they can't ignore:
  It plays a part
  In ev'ry heart
  And ev'ry heart is shouting "Encore!"

REFRAIN

(WARN Blackout.)

Love is sweeping the country;
Waves are hugging the shore;
All the sexes
From Maine to Texas
Have never known such love before.
See them billing and cooing
Like the birdies above.
Each girl and boy alike,
Sharing joy alike
Feels that passion'll
Soon be national.

Love is sweeping the country—
There never was so much love.

(JENKINS, BENSON *and* BOYS *sing one Chorus.* 16 GIRLS (DANCERS) *and* 8 BOYS (SINGERS) *enter* R. *and* L. *on this Chorus.*)

(JENKINS *and* BENSON *dance, the* GIRLS *gesture, the* BOYS *sing one Chorus.*)

(JENKINS *and* BENSON *dance,* GIRLS *and* BOYS *gesture.* **One** *Chorus.*)

(JENKINS, BENSON *and* BOYS *exit* C.)

(GIRLS *dance. One Chorus. Exit* L.)

(JENKINS *and* BENSON *enter* C. *Dance one Chorus. Exit* L.)

BLACKOUT

DRAW CURTAIN

ACT ONE

SCENE VI

Stage LIGHTS up; open Draw Curtain.

Inside Madison Square Garden.
    The lights reveal the interior of the Garden. A speakers' platform, four feet high, stands about ten feet upstage. Leading up to it, both R. *and* L., *are little flights of stairs. On the platform itself, at the back, is a row of seven chairs. The two* C. *chairs are empty; those who occupy the others are* LIPPMAN, GILHOOLEY, JONES *and* LYONS. *The space between the platform and the footlights is bare. The seats in which spectators sit are at Right and Left against walls. Two rows of seats are visible on each side, and one gets the feeling that they extend far off on both sides. As for as the eye can see, of course, they are filled. The scene is in full blast when the Curtains open.*

FULTON. *(At the rostrum as the Curtains open, in the middle of a speech and the middle of a sentence)* —Seventeen Hundred and Seventy-Six, Eighteen Hundred and Twelve, Eighteen Hundred and Sixty-One, Eighteen Hundred and Ninety-Eight, and Nineteen Hundred and Seventeen! *(There is loud APPLAUSE as he stops.)* And so, my friends, on Tuesday next yours is a great privilege. You will cast your ballots for the greatest cause and the greatest emotion known to the heart of mankind! Love! *(APPLAUSE)* Yes, my good friends, for love! For love and for the greatest of all lovers! John P. Wintergreen! *(He sits down C. to great APPLAUSE.)*

LOUD SPEAKER. *(Through the cluster of megaphones that hangs overhead)* Attention, please! Next Wednesday night: Jack Sharkey, American champion of the world, versus Max Schmeling, German champion of the world, in their annual battle for the championship of the world! *(APPLAUSE.)*

FULTON. *(Again to his feet)* And, my friends, as a good American, I believe that Jack Sharkey will win! *(APPLAUSE. He sits.)*

LOUD SPEAKER. Attention, please! Message for Doctor Hugo Kristmacher! Doctor Kristmacher! Your wife has just telephoned the box-office and says not to come home tonight. *(APPLAUSE.)*

FULTON. *(Rises.* JONES *covers face with hand)* And now, my good people, it is my great pleasure and privilege to introduce a man who has served his country long and gloriously, a man who has for many years waged a great and single-handed fight for what he considered his own interests—the silver-tongued orator of the golden West, Senator Carver Crockett Jones! *(APPLAUSE.)*

(JONES *comes forward; shakes hands with the* COMMITTEE. ATTENDANTS *enter* L. *1st entrance, spread mat* C., *then stand* L. *and* R. *of it.)*

LOUD SPEAKER. Attention, please! While Senator Jones is speaking you will be entertained by the world's greatest wrestlers, Vladimir Vidovitch—*(He enters* L.*)*—the Harlem Heaver, and Yussef Yussevitch—*(He enters* R.*)*—the Terrible Turk, in a match for the world's championship. *(APPLAUSE after "Vidovitch" and "Yussevitch." There is the sound of a GONG. Simultaneously the* WRESTLERS *go into action and* SENATOR JONES *starts his speech.* ATTENDANTS *exit* L. *and* R. *with bathrobes.)*

JONES. My friends! We have arrived at a great moment in our history. Magnificent though our past has been, it dwindles into utter insignificance beside the brilliance of our future destiny. Gaze into that future, my friends, and what do you see? What do you see? *(At this moment what one chiefly sees is the rear elevation of* VIDOVITCH *which is being stared at with something akin to admiration by* YUSSEVITCH. *Gradually they draw all eyes, with* LIPPMAN *and* GILHOOLEY *trying discreetly to peer over the edge. They break, and resume wrestling as* JONES *resumes talking)* Not for us the entangling alliances of Europe, not for us the allying entanglances of Asia. *(A burst of APPLAUSE. The* WRESTLERS, *at the moment, have a complicated double scissors hold on each other but their arms are free. Pausing in their labors, they join in the applause.)* Here, then, we stand, alone in our strength, solitary in our splendor, the greatest, the most glorious country that God Almighty put upon earth—the United States of *America! ! ! (The* WRESTLERS, *relinquishing a complicated hold, jump to their feet and salute. The* CROWD *bursts into applause.)* And so, my friends—

(One of the WRESTLERS *makes a sensational dive for the other's legs, throwing him to the mat with a crash. The* CROWD *rises and sets up a cheering and yelling, egging on the* WRESTLERS. *The* COMMITTEE MEN *sitting behind* JONES *crowd to the edge of the rail to look on. The whole* CROWD *is on its feet.* JONES *tries bravely to talk against this for a moment, but his own interest in the* WRESTLERS *finally gets the better of him. He joins the cheerers. The match now turns into real wrestling, with the* CROWD *on high all the time. It comes to a climax as one of the* WRESTLERS *finally gets the other down. The GONG sounds seven or eight times. CHEERS. APPLAUSE. Bows. The* WRESTLERS *exit* R. *and* L. *The* ATTENDANTS *roll up the mat and exit* L. *The* CROWD *settles back.)*

FULTON. *(Is on his feet, ready to speak. There is a HULLABALOO off* L.—*sound of a scuffle, voices, etc. The* CROWD *gets to its feet as the noise mounts. Enter* THROTTLEBOTTOM, L., *trying to fight off* FOUR POLICEMEN. *As he comes into view it is seen that he is practically in tatters, his coat off, his collar askew. He struggles to the foot of the platform stairs.)* Here, here, here! What's all this? Who is this man? Stop that noise! What is this? *(The NOISE quiets down. The* POLICEMEN *stand holding tightly onto* THROTTLEBOTTOM, *two to each arm.)* What is all this? What do you want here?

THROTTLEBOTTOM. *(At the foot of the steps)* But, wait, wait! I'm Throttlebottom! I'm the Vice-President. Here— look! I'm Throttlebottom! *(Takes a banner from his pocket and unrolls it. It bears his picture and reads: "For Vice-President: ALEXANDER THROTTLEBOTTOM.")*

FULTON. Oh, yes! Yes! It's all right, officers. This man is all right! (THROTTLEBOTTOM *gets up on the platform, is trying to get his clothes together, stuffing his shirt into his trousers, getting his collar back on.*) Well, what happened to you?

THROTTLEBOTTOM. They wouldn't let me in.

FULTON. Why didn't you tell 'em who you were?

THROTTLEBOTTOM. I did.

FULTON. Well—?

THROTTLEBOTTOM. That's when they tried to throw me out.

FULTON. *(At the rostrum, reluctantly)* My friends, we have an unexpected surprise for you. It is your great and rare privilege to hear a few words from—(THROTTLEBOTTOM *prompts him*)—Alexander Throttle-something—*(He pronounces the name with great care)*—candidate for—what's it? (THROTTLEBOTTOM *prompts him again, first looking at the banner himself.*) Vice-President—*(Then, as an afterthought)*—of the United States of America. *(Sits* C. *The* CROWD *is silent.* THROTTLEBOTTOM *shows crowd his banner, hands hat to* FULTON, *who passes it to* GILHOOLEY, *who passes it to* LIPPMAN, *who throws it off the platform.* THROTTLEBOTTOM *advances to the rostrum; takes his speech from his pocket. It unrolls all the way to the ground and proves to be about ten feet long. A pleased expression spreads over his face; recognition is his at last.*)

LOUD SPEAKER. *(Just as* THROTTLEBOTTOM *opens his mouth to speak)* Attention, please! (THROTTLEBOTTOM'S *eyes go up to the megaphone)* At the end of the first period in Montreal: Boston Bruins, 3; Chicago White Sox, 1. *(The machine clanks off.* THROTTLEBOTTOM *again gets ready to speak. Once more a slow smile comes over his face; once more he is just about to speak.)* Attention, please! There will now be an intermission of fifteen minutes. *(There is a great pushing back of chairs;* EVERYBODY *gets up and starts to leave.)*

THROTTLEBOTTOM. No, no, no! No!

(The various NOISES on stage merge into a greater and growing noise off stage. Cries of "Wintergreen!" "Here comes Wintergreen!" Those on stage pick the cry up. Enter WINTERGREEN *and* MARY TURNER L., *preceded by the* POLICEMEN. *To the accompaniment of cheers and handshaking they advance to the platform and go up the stairs. There is a great shaking of hands with the* COMMITTEEMEN. THROTTLEBOTTOM, *as the presidential procession gets up onto the platform, is simply pushed right out of the way by the* POLICEMEN *and practically falls down the stairs on the R side. Here he is met again by the*

POLICEMEN, *and is ignominiously dragged out* R., **kicking** *and protesting. Meanwhile, as the noise subsides,* WIN- TERGREEN *and* MARY *take the two* C. *seats that have been left empty for them, and* FULTON *advances to the rostrum to introduce them.)*

FULTON. *(Stilling the tumult with upraised hand)* No need to tell you who the next speakers will be. They are the most beloved couple in America today, the most beloved couple that have ever run for the highest office in the gift of the American people. There have been many great lovers in history. But Romeo never loved Juliet, Dante never loved Beatrice, Damon never loved Pythias, as John P. Wintergreen loves Mary Tur- ner. *(APPLAUSE)* My friends, the issue of this campaign is a simple one. We do not talk to you about war debts or wheat or immigration—we appeal to your hearts; not your intelligence. It is the old, old story, yet ever new—the sweetest story ever told. John P. Wintergreen, candidate for President of the United States, loves Mary Turner. Mary Turner, the most beautiful, the loveliest example of typical American woman- hood—and I defy our opponents to say otherwise—*(Glares at audience)*—loves John P. Wintergreen. He has proposed to her in forty-seven States of the Union, and in forty-seven States she has accepted him. Tonight she will give him her answer in the great Empire State of New York! John and Mary, stand up! *(They do so. APPLAUSE.)* Can you look at them and not be thrilled by their youth, their charm, their pas- sion? Ladies and gentlemen, I give you John P. Wintergreen and Mary Turner! (FULTON *sits down as PANDEMONIUM breaks loose.* WINTERGREEN *and* MARY *come forward; the tu- mult slowly dies.)*

WINTERGREEN. *(The orator)* My friends, I come before you in this final rally of the campaign, not as John P. Winter- green the candidate, not as John P. Wintergreen the statesman, but as a simple man in love. So I beg you to bear with me for a moment, while I ask the girl of my dreams if she will be my heart's delight. *(There is APPLAUSE as he turns to* MARY, *still the orator)* Miss Turner, there has been something on my mind for a long, long time.

MARY. *(Looks away from him)* Yes, Mr. Wintergreen?

WINTERGREEN. *(The hesitant lover)* May I not call you— Mary?

MARY. I wish you would—John.

WINTERGREEN. Do you remember that night we first walked together, on the boardwalk in Atlantic City?

MARY. With the moon shining overhead?

WINTERGREEN. *(Puts arms around her)* And the lights rippling on the water. Do you remember what I said to you, Mary, as I took your dear hand in mine?

MARY. Ah, yes— *(She drops her eyes.)*

WINTERGREEN. And in the cornfields of Kansas, on the plains of Arizona, in the mountains of Nebraska, I whispered to you how much you were beginning to mean to me.

MARY. Our friendship has been a wonderful thing to me.

WINTERGREEN. And in the cave in Kentucky—(Two MEN *come on* L.; *one with camera, other with flash.* WINTERGREEN *stops, and he and* MARY *pose till flash goes off and until picture is taken)*—when you were frightened of the darkness, I put my arm around your trembling shoulder and drew you to me.

(WARN Stage Lights Dim.)

MARY. *(To him)* You were so brave, so strong.

WINTERGREEN. Mary, I can conceal it from you no longer. Look at me. *(She pays no attention—he nudges her)* Look at me! I love you. *(The* CROWD *breaks into great CHEERS and APPLAUSE.* WINTERGREEN *stops them with a gesture)* Yes, Mary, I love you. *(Stops APPLAUSE, which has not come.)*

MARY. Why, John! I hardly know what to say.

WINTERGREEN. Say that you love me, Mary, and that you will be mine.

MARY. I do love you, John. *(APPLAUSE.)*

WINTERGREEN. *(Again checks them)* And if I am elected President, you will marry me?

MARY. *(With simple determination)* I will.

WINTERGREEN. *(Turns quickly to the* CROWD, *his arm still around* MARY) Citizens, it is up to you! Can you let this glorious romance end unhappily!

MARY. Can you tear asunder two loving hearts whom God hath joined together?

WINTERGREEN. I put my faith and trust in the American people! Go, then, to the polls on Tuesday and show the whole world that the United States of America stands first, last and always for Love! Are you with me?

ALL. *(On their feet)* Yes!

(WARN Curtain.)

FULTON. Sing 'em the campaign song, Jack! Sing the campaign love song! *(Another burst of APPLAUSE. The LIGHTS on stage dim, leaving only the ring light on, and a spot on* WINTERGREEN.)

WINTERGREEN. (L.)

Of thee I sing, baby,

Summer, autumn, winter, spring, baby;

You're my silver lining,
You're my sky of blue;
There's a love light shining,
All because of you.
Of thee I sing, baby; *(Crossing* R. *to her)*
You have got that certain thing, baby;
Shining star and inspiration,
Worthy of a mighty nation—
Of thee I sing! *(Takes her* C.*)*
MARY. (C.)
Of thee I sing, baby,
Summer, autumn, winter, spring, baby!
You're my silver lining,
You're my sky of blue,
There's a love light shining,
ALL. *(Coming down to below platform)*
All because of you!
Of thee I sing, baby;
You have got that certain thing, baby!

(ALL *face* WINTERGREEN.*)*

WINTERGREEN.
Shining star and inspiration,
Worthy of a mighty nation—
Of thee I—
ALL. *(Pick it up and face front)*
Of thee I sing, baby,
Summer, autumn, winter, spring, baby!
Shining star and inspiration,
Worthy of a mighty nation—
Of thee I sing!

DRAW CURTAIN CLOSE.

ARC LIGHTS OUT.

ACT ONE

SCENE VII

MOVIE Start. AMPLIFIER Up. Open Draw Curtain.

*A motion picture screen. Election night—the returns.
There is a steady blast of CHEERING and SHOUTING*

that accompanies the picture from beginning to end. There is also, of course, a musical accompaniment.

As the Scene progresses the various items follow each other in quicker and quicker succession, so that a climax is built to and a real pitch of excitement achieved.

Herewith the sequence.

WHITESIDE, VERMONT.
Indications are that WINTERGREEN *has swept the town by a plurality of* 154.

WATERVILLE, MASS.
Early returns show WINTERGREEN *well ahead. First elec- tion district gives:*
  WINTERGREEN 12
  Scattering 1

JOHN P. WINTERGREEN *(Picture).*

MARY TURNER *(Picture).*

ATLANTA, GA.

16 *election districts out of* 184 *give:*
  WINTERGREEN 12,736
  JEFFERSON DAVIS 1,653

NEW YORK, N. Y.
  126 *election districts report:*
  WINTERGREEN 72,639
  BRYAN 128
  Absent 4
  Late 2

MARY TURNER *(Picture).*

JOHN P. WINTERGREEN *(Picture).*

GEORGE WASHINGTON *(Picture).*

LANDSLIDE, NEB.
  JOHN P. WINTERGREEN 12,538
  A Man Named WILKINS......... 1

PATRICK HENRY *(Picture).*

HOLLYWOOD, CAL.
          WINTERGREEN 160,000
          MICKEY MOUSE 159,000
          GLORIA SWANSON'S FIRST HUSBAND 84,638

Caption: Candidate JOHN P. WINTERGREEN *casting Ballot No. 8 at Public School 63 at 6:05 o'clock this morning. Picture of* WINTERGREEN *casting ballot.*

Same picture of WINTERGREEN *casting ballot. Caption: Candidate* JOHN P. WINTERGREEN *casting Ballot No. 168 at Public School 145 at 8:10 o'clock this morning and 2:25 this afternoon.*

NEW YORK, N. Y.
     ALEXANDER THROTTLEBOTTOM, *vice-presidential candidate, gets his shoes shined preparatory to entering election booth.*
     (Picture of a pair of hands shining a pair of shoes. The candidate is not visible above the knees.)

THE WHITE HOUSE *(Picture).*

JOHN P. WINTERGREEN *(Picture).*

J. P. WINTERGREEN *at the age of 5 years (Picture).*

DEAL, N. J.
     Returns from Contract Bridge Tournament give:
          WINTERGREEN 1,500
          CULBERTSON .... Double
          LENZ .... Redouble
          THROTTLEBOTTOM .... Pass

BENJAMIN FRANKLIN *(Picture).*

BABE RUTH *(Picture).*

NEW YORK, N. Y.
     41 *Election Districts give:*
          WINTERGREEN 46,572
          WALTER HAMPDEN   136
          MAE WEST   82

LEXINGTON, KENTUCKY.
          WINTERGREEN   27,637

LIGHT WINES AND BEER 14
STRAIGHT WHISKEY 1,850,827

JOHN P. WINTERGREEN *(Picture)*.

PATRICK HENRY *(Picture)*.

JACK DEMPSEY *(Picture)*.

MAN O' WAR *(Picture)*.

MANCHESTER, ENGLAND.
WINTERGREEN 14,653
KING GEORGE 3
QUEEN MARY 1
ALSO RAN ....NURMI

ROME, ITALY.
127 *Election Districts give:*
WINTERGREEN 0
MUSSOLINI 828,638

NEW YORK.
Empire State gives WINTERGREEN *plurality of* 1,627,535, *with only three counties missing.*

DETROIT, MICH.
New eight-cylinder Ford gives WINTERGREEN *huge plurality with only two cylinders missing.*

TOLEDO, OHIO.
Twelfth National Bank gives WINTERGREEN *plurality with all its cashiers missing.*

GEORGE WASHINGTON *(Picture)*.

THE MARX BROTHERS *(Picture)*.

NEW YORK, N. Y.
First returns from Wall Street give:
WINTERGREEN 192,000
RADIO 5¾
GOLDMAN, SACHS 2⅛

THE WHITE HOUSE *(Picture)*.

THE CAPITOL *(Picture)*.

THE ROXY *(Picture)*.

ROXY HIMSELF *(Picture)*.

A FRIEND OF ROXY'S *(Picture)*.

AN UNIDENTIFIED MAN *(Picture of* THROTTLEBOTTOM*)*.

MACY'S BASEMENT.
      WINTERGREEN .... ~~$1.50~~ 97c
          Only One to a Customer

RICHMOND, VA.
      WINTERGREEN 98,728
      MASON   499
      DIXON   1
      MASON & DIXON   500

        All returns indicate that WINTERGREEN
             is sweeping country!

         WINTERGREEN *lacks only four votes*
              to win!
                  (WARN Draw Curtain.)

WINTERGREEN CASTS LAST FOUR VOTES

         W I N T E R G R E E N
            E L E C T E D !

OUR NEXT PRESIDENT *(Picture)*.

OUR NEXT FIRST LADY *(Picture)*.

BULLETIN: *At a late hour tonight the defeated candidate*
sent the following telegram to JOHN P. WINTERGREEN,
the winner:
"Heartily congratulate you on your splendid victory and
charge fraud in Indiana, Illinois, Nebraska, Montana,
Washington, Ohio and Massachusetts."

BULLETIN: *At midnight tonight* ALEXANDER THROTTLEBOT-
TOM *refused to concede his election as Vice-President.*

Next Week:
NORMA SHEARER
(Picture)
in
"THE LOVE GIRL"

Flash of Metro-Golywyn-Mayer lion.
It opens its mouth. It crows.

CLOSE DRAW CURTAIN.

LIGHTS UP.

ACT ONE

SCENE VIII

Open Draw Curtain.

SCENE: *The steps of the Capitol. Inauguration Day. The steps begin as close to the footlights as possible. Three steps up there is a platform about six feet deep, with space for entrances R. and L. There are twelve steps above this, with another platform, rather narrow, at the top of these. Where the steps end the idea of steps is carried out by a painted back drop, which also shows the Capitol building itself and its great dome. At R. and L. downstage are huge pillars. Upstage, wings R. and L. and borders above are painted to represent flags and bunting. Ground rows R. and L. show an immense crowd, of which nothing can be seen but masses of umbrellas.*

AT RISE: *16 GIRLS enter R. and L. in red uniforms, with tall, feather head-dresses. They are followed by 16 BOYS in blue and white military uniforms. All carry silvered batons. They go through a short drill to the music of "WINTER-GREEN FOR PRESIDENT," and finish on the upper steps in fan-shaped formation.*

The 9 SUPREME COURT JUSTICES enter R., come to the C. of the platform, and sing, the CHIEF JUSTICE in the C.

JUSTICES.
   We're the one, two, three, four, five, six, seven, eight, nine
      Supreme Court Judges;
   As the Super Solomons of this great nation;
   We will supervise today's Inauguration,
   And we'll sup'rintend the wedding celebration
   In a manner official and judicial.
ALL.
   One, two, three, four, five, six, seven, eight, nine Supreme
      Court Judges!
JUSTICES.
   We have powers that are positively regal;
   Only we can take a law and make it legal.
ALL.
   They're (we're) the A.K.'s who give the O.K.'s!
   One, two, three, four, five, six, seven, eight, nine Supreme
      Court Judges!

(Another FANFARE.)

ALL.
   Hail, hail, the mighty ruler of love!
   Hail, hail, the man who made us love love!
   Hip, hip, hooray,
   For his Inaugural and wedding day—
   Hurray!

(JUSTICES *drop off platform* R. *and* L. *CHEERS from* ALL.
   Enter WINTERGREEN, *followed by* COMMITTEE *and* JEN-
   KINS R.)

   CHIEF JUSTICE. (L.C.) And, now, Mr. President, if you
don't mind, we'd like your Inaugural address.
   WINTERGREEN.
      I have definite ideas about the Philippines
      And the herring situation up in Bismarck;
      I have notions on the salaries of movie queens,
      And the men who sign their signatures with *this* mark!
         (Makes cross.)
   ALL.
      He has definite ideas about the Philippines
      And the herring situation up in Bismarck;
      He has notions on the salaries of movie queens,
      And the men who sign their signatures with this mark!
         (Make cross.)

WINTERGREEN.
But on this glorious day I find
I'm sentimentally inclined,
And so—
I sing this to the girls I used to know:
Here's a kiss for Cinderella,
And a parting kiss for May;
Toodle-oo, goodbye! This is my wedding day!
Here's a parting glance for Della,
And the lady known as Lou;

(5 JUSTICES over L. *back of* SHOWGIRLS.)

Toodle-oo, goodbye! With bach'lor days I'm through!
Though I really never knew them,
It's a rule I must obey;
I am singing goodbye to them
In the customary way.
My regards to Arabella.
And to Emmaline and Kay;
Toodle-oo, dear girls, goodbye! This is my wedding day!

(He repeats the first six lines, the COMMITTEE *joining in—all*
OTHERS *sing the counter melody.)*

ALL.
He is toodle-ooing all his lady loves,
All the girls he didn't know so well;
All the innocent and all the shady loves—
Oh, dinga donga dell!
Bride and groom! Their future should be glorious!
What a happy story they will tell!
Let the welkin now become uproarious—
Oh, dinga donga, dinga donga dell!

(Elevator up. ALL *turn to greet* MARY, *who appears top of
steps,* C.)

ALL.
Clear the way!
Hail the bride!
Sweet and gay—
Here comes the bride!
MARY. *(Coming down steps)*
Is it true or am I dreaming?

Do I go to Heav'n to stay?
Never was a girl so happy on her wedding day!

(MARY *and* WINTERGREEN *now on lower platform. MUSIC continues.*)

CHIEF JUSTICE. Do you, John P. Wintergreen, solemnly swear to uphold the Constitution of the United States of America and to love, honor and cherish this woman so long as you two shall live?

WINTERGREEN. I do.

CHIEF JUSTICE. Do you, Mary Turner, promise to love, honor and cherish this man as long as you two shall live?

MARY. I do.

CHIEF JUSTICE. Therefore, by virtue of the power that is vested in me as Chief Justice, I hereby pronounce you President of the United States, man and wife.

WINTERGREEN. Mary!

MARY. John! *(They embrace.)*

ALL. Hurray!

BOTH.

Is it true or am I dreaming?
Do I go to Heav'n to stay?
Never was a girl (man) so happy on her (his) wedding—
(Discord in orchestra. DIANA *appears L.)*

DIANA. Stop! Halt! Pause! Wait!

ALL.

Who is this intruder?
There's no one could be ruder!

(To DIANA*)*

What's your silly notion
In causing this commotion?

DIANA. *(Recitative)* I was the most beautiful blossom in all the Southland. I was sent up North to enter the contest, with the understanding that the winner was to be the President's wife. The Committee examined me. My lily white body fascinated them. I was chosen. It was the happiest moment of my life.

ALL. *(Excepting, of course,* MARY, JOHN *and* COMMITTEE*)* Yes, yes, go on! Yes, yes, go on!

DIANA. Suddenly the sky fell—suddenly for no reason at all, no reason at all, this man rejected me. All my castles came tumbling down. And so I am serving him with a summons—for breach of promise!

ALL.
  What! What!
  The water's getting hot!
  She says he made a promise—
  A promise he forgot!
DIANA. It's true! It's true! *(Crossing* L.)
CHIEF JUSTICE.
  The day he's getting married
  You put him on the spot!
ALL.
  It's dirty work of Russia—
  A communistic plot!
WINTERGREEN.
  Please understand. It wasn't that I would jilt or spurn 'er;
  It's just that there was someone else—
ALL. Whom?
WINTERGREEN. Who! Mary Turner! *(Crossing* R. *to her.)*
CHIEF JUSTICE.
  We're having fits!
ALL.
  They're having fits!
CHIEF JUSTICE.
  The man admits
ALL.
  The man admits
CHIEF JUSTICE.
  This little sinner
ALL.
  This little sinner
CHIEF JUSTICE.
  Was really winner!
ALL.
  Was really winner!
DIANA.
  I couldn't see
ALL.
  She couldn't see
DIANA.
  His jilting me,
ALL.
  His jilting she,
DIANA.
  And so I'm doing
ALL.
  And so she's doing

DIANA.
  A bit of suing.
ALL.
  A bit of suing.
MEN.
  And if it's true she has a claim,
  You should be called a dirty name!
GIRLS.
  Yes, if it's true she has a claim,
  Then you're a dirty, dirty name!
MARY. (R.C.)
  John, no matter what they do to hurt you, *(Takes his hand)*
  The one you love won't desert you.
DIANA. (C.)
  I'm a queen who lost her king;
  Why should she wear the wedding ring? *(Crossing L.)*
WINTERGREEN. (C.)
  Some girls can bake a pie, *(Crossing L.)*
  Made up of prunes and quinces,
  Some make an oyster fry—
  Others are good at blintzes.
  Some lovely girls have done
  Wonders with turkey stuffin's,
  But I have found the one
  Who can really make corn muffins! *(Crosses to MARY.)*
ALL.
  Yes, he has found the one
  Who can really make corn muffins.

                            (WARN Curtain.)

DIANA. *(Crossing L.)*
  Who cares about corn muffins?
  All I demand is justice.
WINTERGREEN *and* MARY. *(To* JUSTICES*)*
  Which is more important—corn muffins or justice?
ALL.
  Which is more important—corn muffins or justice?
CHIEF JUSTICE. (C. *of platform. Speaks)* If you will wait a moment—you'll have our decision. Forty—seven—eleven—

(The JUSTICES *leap into a football huddle. Music agitato. After a moment they resume positions.)*

CHIEF JUSTICE. The decision of the Supreme Court is— Corn Muffins!

ALL.
Great! Great! (SHOWGIRLS *on steps.*)
It's written on the slate!
There's none but Mary Turner
Could ever be his mate!

DIANA. (C.)
It's I, not Mary Turner,
Who should have been his mate;
I'm off to tell my story
In ev'ry single state! *(Exits L.)*

CHIEF JUSTICE. *(Chasing DIANA off L.)*
Be off with you, young woman,
He's married to his mate!
Be off with you, young woman,
He's married to his mate!

ALL.
There's none but Mary Turner
Could ever be his mate!
There's none but Mary Turner
Could ever be his mate!

WINTERGREEN.
Of thee I sing, baby,

ALL.
Summer, autumn, winter, spring, baby—
Shining star and inspiration,
Worthy of a mighty nation,
Of thee I sing!

CURTAIN.

ACT TWO

Scene I

It is the President's office, in the White House. Not only is it the office of the President, however, but it is also the office of the First Lady, and the room reflects the fact that it is a joint affair. The Presidential desk, for example, is divided into two parts; one L. piled high with various state papers, the other R. lined with perfumes, powders and other perquisites of femininity. Mary's half of the desk is really a dressing table, and stands on gracefully curved legs, whereas the President's half is a solid piece of office furniture.

The door at L. leads to the outer offices, and through it come all visitors. Another door, at the R., leads to the more private portions of the White House. At the rear is a window through which can be seen the Capitol and Washington's Monument.

The desk, set at an angle, is R. of C. There are various comfortable chairs L.C. and up R. and L. for possible visitors.

At Rise: *The Scene opens with a Number, done by* 12 Presidential Secretaries (Boys) *and* 12 *of* Mary's Secretaries (Girls, *of course*). *Each group is led by a* Chief Secretary—*a man and a woman—who turn out to be* Jenkins *and* Miss Benson.

(12 Boy Secretaries *enter* L., 12 Girl Secretaries *enter* R., *whistling.*)

Boys.
  Hello, good morning—
Girls.
  Good morning, hello.
Boys.
  How are you this very lovely day?

57

GIRLS.
    I feel very well, sir.
BOYS.
    And I'm feeling swell.
BOTH.
    It's great to be alive,
    And work from nine to five—

(Enter JENKINS *and* MISS BENSON L.*)*

JENKINS *and* BENSON.
    Hello, good morning—
GIRLS *and* BOYS.
    Good morning, hello.
    Isn't this a morning that's divine?
JENKINS *and* BENSON.
    I see it's almost nine.
ALL.
    And we only have one minute more to say:
    Hello, good morning,
    Isn't this a lovely day?
    Isn't this a lovely day?
ALL.
    Oh, it's great to be a secret'ry
    In the White House, D. C.
    You get inside information on Algeria;
    You know ev'ry move they're making in Liberia.
    You learn what's what and what is not
    In the land of the free.
    Ev'ry corner that you turn you meet a notable
    With a statement that is eminently quotable—
    Oh, it's great to be a secret'ry
    In the White House, D. C.

(JENKINS *and* BENSON *dance,* BOYS *and* GIRLS *gesture. At conclusion of dance* BOYS *and* GIRLS *and* JENKINS *and* BENSON *exit* R., *arm in arm, singing:)*

    So long, good morning;
    Wasn't this a lovely day?
    Wasn't this a lovely day?

(They whistle as they exit.)

(As the SECRETARIES *exit* R. *the* L. *door opens and a* GUIDE *enters, followed by a crowd of ten* SIGHTSEERS. *The* SIGHT-

SEERS *are plainly from the country, with loosely wrapped umbrellas, women with waistlines not in the right place, and perhaps a terrible child or two. The voice of the* GUIDE *is heard as the door opens.)*

GUIDE. And this, ladies and gentlemen, is the executive office. This is the room in which the President discharges his official duties, and has been occupied by every President since Hoover. On your right stands the famous double desk used by the President and Mrs. Wintergreen in administering the affairs of the country. During the 1912 coal shortage this room was used as a garage. Right this way, please. *(Opens door at* R.*)* We are now entering the room from which, on a historic occasion, the Spanish Ambassador jumped out of the window, in the very nick of time. *(Going through door, with* CROWD *following. The PHONE rings.* JENKINS *enters* L.*; crosses to desk.)* Here the diplomatic corps gathers once a month to pay its formal respects to the Chief Executive, and here, too, the cabinet assembles when— *(The last* SIGHTSEER *is through the door. It closes.)*

JENKINS. *(At phone)* Hello. Who? No, the Coolidges don't live here any more! (MISS BENSON *enters* R.*)* Gosh, I can't do these dances every morning.

MISS BENSON. *(Holding a perfume bottle up to the light)* Mrs. Wintergreen is running low on Chanel Number Five.

JENKINS. *(Consulting paper)* Looks like a pretty full day. *(Reads)* Delegation from South America—

MISS BENSON. What's eating them?

JENKINS. Usual thing. Want Hollywood cleaned up. *(Looking at list)* Delegation of Camisole Indians—they want scalping restored. Committee of cotton manufacturers—that's for Mrs. Wintergreen. They want her to bring back cotton stockings.

MISS BENSON. Oh, they do, eh?

JENKINS. *(Consulting schedule)* Mayors of fourteen American cities— (SECOND SECRETARY *enters* L.*, with newspaper clippings.)* Well?

SECOND SECRETARY. Morning editorials. *(Hands over clippings; goes.* JENKINS *looks the clippings over; shakes his head.)*

MISS BENSON. What's the matter?

JENKINS. Same thing. They're still harping on it.

MISS BENSON. You mean Devereaux?

JENKINS. *(As he reads)* Mm.

MISS BENSON. What's it say?

JENKINS. Nothing new. They just think she got a raw deal.

MISS BENSON. A lot of people think that.

JENKINS. *(Crumpling a clipping)* Just as well if he doesn't see this one. You know, it wouldn't surprise me a bit— (THIRD SECRETARY *enters.)*

THIRD SECRETARY. Mr. Jenkins—

JENKINS. Yes?

THIRD SECRETARY. Those people are here now. Can you see them?

JENKINS. *(A gesture to R.)* Show them into the Blue Room.

THIRD SECRETARY. Yes, sir. *(Goes.)*

JENKINS. *(Crossing R.)* Delegation from the Virgin Islands. Want to come along?

MISS BENSON. *(To side of desk)* Well, well! And what are they after?

JENKINS. *(Dropping below desk)* Want their name changed. They claim it's hurting business. (MISS BENSON *exits R., followed by* JENKINS.)

(GUIDE *enters L. again, leading another sightseeing party. It is the same sort of group as the first, except that included in it, although not visible in the beginning, is* ALEXANDER THROTTLEBOTTOM.)

GUIDE. Right this way, please—follow me. This, ladies and gentlemen, is the executive office. You will probably find this the most interesting room in your entire tour of the White House. It is in this room that the President signs the many laws that govern your everyday life, and from which he controls the various departmental activities. (THROTTLEBOTTOM, *all eyes, emerges a bit from the crowd. He is gaping at the room, taking in every detail.)* Here come the various heads of government for daily consultation with the Executive, and to receive from him the benefit of his wide experience. It is in this room— *(To* THROTTLEBOTTOM, *who has strayed about ten feet from the group)* I beg your pardon, sir, but would you please stay over there? You see, we're personally responsible if anything's stolen.

THROTTLEBOTTOM. *(Meekly rejoining the group)* Yes, sir.

GUIDE. Thank you. *(Resuming his formal tone)* Now, are there any questions?

FIRST SIGHTSEER. Does the President live here all year round?

GUIDE. All year round. Except when Congress is in session.

FIRST SIGHTSEER. Where does the Vice-President live?

GUIDE. Who?

FIRST SIGHTSEER. The Vice-President. Where does he live?

GUIDE. *(Taking a little red book out of his pocket)* Just one moment, please. Vice-regent, viceroy, vice societies— I'm sorry, but he doesn't seem to be in here.

THROTTLEBOTTOM. I can tell you about that.

GUIDE. What?

THROTTLEBOTTOM. I know where the Vice-President lives.

GUIDE. Where?

THROTTLEBOTTOM. He lives at fourteen forty-eight Z Street. *(To the* SIGHTSEER*)* It's the next to the last house, 'way down at the other end of Z Street.

GUIDE. Well, that's very interesting. He has a house there, has he?

THROTTLEBOTTOM. Well, he lives there.

GUIDE. All by himself?

THROTTLEBOTTOM. No, with the other boarders. It's an awfully nice place. Mrs. Spiegelbaum's. It's a great place, if you like Kosher cooking.

GUIDE. Think of your knowing all that! Are you a Washingtonian?

THROTTLEBOTTOM. Well, I've been here since March fourth. I came down for the Inauguration, but I lost the ticket.

GUIDE. You don't say? Well! First time you've been to the White House?

THROTTLEBOTTOM. *(Nods)* I didn't know people were allowed in.

GUIDE. You seem to know the Vice-President pretty well. What kind of fellow is he?

THROTTLEBOTTOM. He's all right. He's a nice fellow when you get to know him, but nobody wants to know him.

GUIDE. What's the matter with him?

THROTTLEBOTTOM. There's nothing the matter with him. Nothing. He's just Vice-President.

GUIDE. Well, what does he do all the time?

THROTTLEBOTTOM. He sits around in the parks, and feeds the pigeons, and takes walks, and goes to the movies. And the other day he was going to join the library, but he had to have two references, so he couldn't get in.

GUIDE. But when does he do all his work?

THROTTLEBOTTOM. What work?

FIRST SIGHTSEER. Doesn't he preside over the Senate?

THROTTLEBOTTOM. What?

GUIDE. Sure he does! That's the Vice-President's job!

THROTTLEBOTTOM. What is?

GUIDE. To preside over the Senate.

THROTTLEBOTTOM. *(Coming C.)* Over what?

GUIDE. The Senate. You know what Senators are, don't you?

THROTTLEBOTTOM. Sure. —I saw them play yesterday.

GUIDE. No, no! The Vice-President presides over the Senate. It meets in the Capitol.

THROTTLEBOTTOM. When does it?

GUIDE. Right now! It's going on now!

THROTTLEBOTTOM. *(Frenzied)* How do you get there?

GUIDE. The Capitol?

THROTTLEBOTTOM. Yeah!

GUIDE. Street car at the door—right up Pennsylvania Avenue.

THROTTLEBOTTOM. *(Hurrying off* L.*)* Street car at the door —right up Pennsyl— *(Turns back)* —What's the name of that place?

GUIDE. The Senate! (THROTTLEBOTTOM *dashes off* L.*)*

GUIDE. *(Going* R.*)* Right this way, please. *(Opens door. As the* SIGHTSEERS *reach* C. *there is a fanfare in the orchestra.)* Here the diplomatic corps gather monthly to pay its formal respects to the Chief Executive, and here, too, the cabinet assembles upon the occasion of its weekly meetings. *(The* SIGHTSEERS *and the* GUIDE *are off* R.*)*

(JENKINS *and* MISS BENSON *have entered from* L. MISS BENSON *first—on the fanfare. At its conclusion and as the last of the* SIGHTSEERS *exit,* WINTERGREEN *and* MARY *enter* R. JENKINS *and* MISS BENSON *are standing at attention at their respective chairs.)*

WINTERGREEN *and* MARY. Good morning!

JENKINS *and* MISS BENSON. Good morning! *(As* WINTERGREEN *reaches his chair, the PHONE rings; he answers it.)*

WINTERGREEN. *(In phone)* Hello—no—no—no. *(Hangs up. To* JENKINS*)* Make a note of that.

JENKINS. Yes, sir.

(MARY *is seated at her desk, going through letters.* WINTERGREEN *looks out the window, through which is visible the panorama of Washington, with Washington's Monument prominent in the foreground.)*

WINTERGREEN. What a country—what a country! Jenkins, what monument is that?

JENKINS. *(Disgustedly)* Grant's Tomb.

WINTERGREEN. Oh, yes. Well, what's on the schedule this morning? Ah, here we are! *(Takes up some letters, paces up and down)* Tell the Secretary of the Navy to scrap two battleships.

JENKINS. What?

WINTERGREEN. Tell him to scrap two battleships. Scrap two and build four. Disarmament.

JENKINS. Oh, yes, sir.

WINTERGREEN. Cablegram to the President of San Domingo: "Congratulations on beginning your second day in office. That's five dollars I owe you, and will bet you double or nothing on tomorrow."

JENKINS. Yes, sir.

WINTERGREEN. Tell the Secretary of War to stand ready to collect that bet.

JENKINS. Yes, sir.

WINTERGREEN. Letter to the Friars' Club, Forty-eighth Street, New York City. "Dear Brother Friars: Regret very much I cannot take part in this year's minstrel show. Owing to conditions in the South, I do not think it would be wise for me to black up." *(Goes to the desk, looks through mail)* I get the lousiest mail for a President!

MARY. Emily—take a letter to the A. and P. "Atlantic and Pacific Tea Stores, ladies and gentlemen: I have your bill for eighty-two sixty-three for eggs, for the month of April. One of the eggs delivered on April fifteenth arrived in bad condition and has shown no improvement since that date. I must refuse to pay this bill until you send a new egg, or have the old one attended to." That's all. (BENSON *exits* L. *To* WINTERGREEN) They're not going to put anything over on me.

WINTERGREEN. That's telling 'em. Jenkins!

JENKINS. Yes, sir.

WINTERGREEN. Take a memo to the Secretary of State: "Referring to last Tuesday night's poker game, please note that the Liberian minister's check for twelve dollars and forty-five cents has been returned for lack of funds. Kindly get a new minister for next Tuesday night's game, and add twelve dollars and forty-five cents to the Liberian National Debt."

JENKINS. Yes, sir.

WINTERGREEN. *(Takes* JENKINS *downstage out of earshot* of MARY) Get the Governor of Maryland on the phone and ask him what horse he likes in the fourth race at Pimlico.

JENKINS. Yes, sir.

WINTERGREEN. *(Brandishing a telephone bill)* And tell the telephone company that this is not my bill. *(Hands it to* SECRETARY) That long-distance call was March third.

JENKINS. Yes, sir.

WINTERGREEN. *(As* JENKINS *starts to go)* Oh, anybody in the ante-room?

JENKINS. Yes, sir. Secretary of the Navy, Secretary of Agriculture, and four zebras.

WINTERGREEN. Zebras?

JENKINS. There's a man who wants to give them to you.

WINTERGREEN. Not unless they're housebroken.

(A SECRETARY *enters* L. *with a wooden board, about two feet square, covered with electric buttons. A long wire is attached to the board, and stretches across the stage as the* SECRETARY *advances to* JENKINS.*)*

JENKINS. All ready, Mr. President. *(Takes the board. The* SECRETARY *exits* L.*)* Time to press a button. Opening of the International Corn Growing Exposition in Dubuque, Iowa. Button Number One.

WINTERGREEN. *(Presses button, then laughs)* Say, Jenkins, I never will forget the time 1 reopened the Bank of United States by mistake. *(*BOTH *laugh boisterously;* WINTERGREEN *slaps* JENKINS *on the back;* JENKINS, *a moment later, returns the slap considerably harder.* WINTERGREEN *straightens, freezes;* JENKINS *beats a hasty retreat. The PHONE rings.)* Hello— *(Annoyed, hands instrument to* MARY*)* For you!

MARY. Who is it?

WINTERGREEN. The butcher!

MARY. Hello! Oh, good morning, Mr. Schneidermann. Fine, thank you. Now, let me see. What have you got that's good? Well, we had lamb chops yesterday. They are? Well, wait a minute. *(To* WINTERGREEN*)* John, who's coming to dinner tonight?

WINTERGREEN. What? Let me see—the Chief Justice, the Attorney General, Jackie Cooper, and those three judges that got paroled. That's six.

MARY. *(As she returns to phone)* That's eight with us. Hello, Mr. Schneidermann. Make it sixteen lamb chops—

WINTERGREEN. Wait a minute! What about that moving-picture train from Hollywood.

MARY. That what?

WINTERGREEN. That moving picture train from Hollywood. If that gets in we've got to have *them.*

MARY. Oh, dear! How many are there?

WINTERGREEN. Ah—sixty-four motion picture stars—there may be two actors among them. That's sixty-six.

MARY. That's seventy-four in all.

WINTERGREEN. But they may not get here.

MARY. But when'll we know? Just a minute, Mr. Schneider-mann. *(Back to* WINTERGREEN, *pretty testily)* I've got to know whether they're going to get here.

WINTERGREEN. How do I know? Take a chance! You can always use lamb chops.

MARY. *(Back to phone, wearily)* Listen, Mr. Schneider-mann. A hundred and forty-eight lamb chops. That's right. Now, how is your asparagus? Well, make it a carload of asparagus, and about seventy-five loaves of rye bread. That's all, thank you. *(Hangs up.)*

JENKINS. *(Enters* L.*)* Beg pardon, sir. Time to press another button.

WINTERGREEN. What's this? Button Number Two. Opening of a new speakeasy on Fifty-second Street, New York. *(Presses button)* Wait a minute, Jenkins— Didn't I open that yesterday?

JENKINS. Yes, sir. This is the reopening. It was closed last night. *(Exits* L.*)*

MARY. *(Coming to* WINTERGREEN *with a stack of bills in her hand)* John, look at these grocery bills!

WINTERGREEN. Well, what about it?

MARY. I've simply got to have a bigger allowance.

WINTERGREEN. Again! For God's sake, Mary!

MARY. Well, I can't help it. Fifty people to dinner every night. And Senators to breakfast every morning. It mounts up.

WINTERGREEN. I've got to have them. It's business.

MARY. Then you've got to give me enough to feed them.

WINTERGREEN. Where am I going to get it from?

MARY. Get it from! If you had any gumption you'd ask Congress for a raise.

WINTERGREEN. Ask Congress for a raise! I'm lucky they don't lay me off! *(*JENKINS *enters* L.*)*

JENKINS. I beg your pardon. The Secretary of Agriculture and the Secretary of the Navy are still waiting.

WINTERGREEN. I forgot. Have them come in.

JENKINS. The Secretary of Agriculture! *(Enter* LIPP-MAN L.*)*

LIPPMAN. Hello, Jack! Hello, Mary! ⎫
WINTERGREEN. Hello, Secretary!   ⎬   *(Together)*
JENKINS. The Secretary of the Navy! ⎭

(Enter GILHOOLEY L. JENKINS *withdraws* L.*)*

GILHOOLEY. Mr. President! And Mary!

MARY. Mr. Secretary!

WINTERGREEN. Sit down, boys. Sorry I kept you waiting. } *(Together)*

LIPPMAN. That's all right.

GILHOOLEY. O.K., Chief.

WINTERGREEN. Well, what's on your mind, Louis? How's agriculture?

LIPPMAN. That's what I came to talk to you about. Listen, Jack! I don't know anything about agriculture. I told you I wanted the Treasury.

WINTERGREEN. What's the matter with agriculture?

LIPPMAN. Agriculture's all right— It's those farmers. Wheat, wheat! All they know is raise wheat! And then they raise hell with me because nobody wants it.

WINTERGREEN. Why do you let them raise so much?

LIPPMAN. How can you stop 'em? I did all I could. I invited the seven-year locusts, but they didn't come. Even the locusts don't want their lousy wheat. And they're always complaining about being in one place all the time. —They want to travel.

GILHOOLEY. You call that trouble? How'd you like to have a lot of sailors on your neck?

WINTERGREEN. What do *they* want—*two* wives in every port?

GILHOOLEY. Yeah. And any port in a storm. And no more storms. And another thing—they won't stand for those bells any more. They want to know what time it is the same as anybody else. But that's not the big thing.

WINTERGREEN. Well?

GILHOOLEY. It's the ocean. They don't like the ocean.

WINTERGREEN. *(Rises)* Which ocean don't they like?

GILHOOLEY. All of them. They say it's a nice place to visit, but they don't want to live there. It's no place to bring up a family.

WINTERGREEN. The farmers want to travel and the sailors want to settle down. I've got it! Have them change places!

LIPPMAN. What?

WINTERGREEN. It'll solve the whole problem. Sailors don't know anything about farming—in two years there won't *be* any wheat. You'll have a wheat shortage.

LIPPMAN. And I'll get hell again.

WINTERGREEN. And look what it does for business. You get the farmers on the boats; the traveling salesmen will come back to the farmhouses—you know, to stay over night. Why, I haven't heard a good story in years.

GILHOOLEY. Say, Louis, I wouldn't be surprised if he's got hold of something. That's not a bad idea, Mr. President; not a bad idea at all. That's pretty darned good.

LIPPMAN. The farmers won't like it. I tell you don't know those boys. You know what I think of them?

WINTERGREEN. Just bring your troubles to me, boys; I'll fix them up! Anything else, boys? Anything at all.

MARY. John, I think that's the most wonderful idea I ever heard!

(Together)

(A SECRETARY *enters* L.*)*

SECRETARY. The Secretary of State! (FULTON *strides in* L.*; the* SECRETARY *withdraws. They* ALL *greet him. "Hello, Matty!" "Hi, Sec!")*

FULTON. Hello, boys. Everybody.

WINTERGREEN. How are you, Matty?

FULTON. *(Preoccupied)* What are you doing, Jack? Important?

WINTERGREEN. Just chinning.

FULTON. *(A look toward the doors)* Can you keep the room clear for a little while?

WINTERGREEN. Sure. What's up?

FULTON. *(Starts toward* L. *door)* Shall I tell 'em?

WINTERGREEN. No, here we are. *(Presses a buzzer.)*

LIPPMAN. *(Crossing* GILHOOLEY. *Starting off)* See you later. *(*JENKINS *enters* L.*)*

FULTON. No, no. Want you fellows to stay.

WINTERGREEN. I don't want to be disturbed for a little while.

JENKINS. Yes, sir.

FULTON. Just a minute. When Senators Jones and Lyons get here, bring 'em in.

JENKINS. Yes, sir.

FULTON. And nobody else.

JENKINS. Yes, sir. What shall I do about the press conference?

FULTON. Have 'em wait! *(*JENKINS *exits* L. FULTON *waits for the doors to close and crosses to* WINTERGREEN. GILHOOLEY *and* LIPPMAN *drop down.)* There's hell to pay!

WINTERGREEN. What's the matter?

FULTON. Devereaux!

MARY. John!

WINTERGREEN. *(He puts an arm around her)* What about her?

FULTON. *(To* LIPPMAN *and* GILHOOLEY*)* The thing has been growing for weeks—you know that, boys—

WINTERGREEN. What has?

FULTON. Well, you know there's always been a certain bunch that said Devereaux didn't get a square deal.

WINTERGREEN. A handful of Southerners.

FULTON. At the beginning. And now it's spreading all over the country!

WINTERGREEN. What do you mean?

MARY. What's happened?

FULTON. I'll tell you what I mean. Yesterday the Federation of New Jersey Woman's Clubs came out solid for Devereaux.

MARY. John! *(A sob from her.* GILHOOLEY *whistles, crosses up and to* R., *followed by* LIPPMAN *at end of desk.)*

FULTON. And this morning I get a petition from the Kansas City Elks—demanding Devereaux! And the same thing'll happen with the Moose and the Shriners! *(Enter* SENATORS JONES *and* LYONS L.*)*

JONES. Mr. President! Good morning, Mary.

LYONS. Good morning, suh!—and Mary! *(A nod or two from the* OTHERS.*)*

FULTON. Good! I've just been telling the President how things stand! *(Crosses down* R.*)*

JONES. Mr. President, I cannot overstate the case. The West is up in arms.

LYONS. The South, suh, is on fire!

JONES. Nebraska has just declared martial law! A posse has been formed!

LYONS. In Louisiana you have been hanged in effigy!

WINTERGREEN. *(Defiant)* How do the Philippines feel about it? (JONES *and* LYONS *go up stage.)*

MARY. It's all my fault.

WINTERGREEN. I'd rather have you than Nebraska.

FULTON. It doesn't matter whose fault it is. We've got to do something. We've got to do something to counteract this Devereaux propaganda.

WINTERGREEN. *(Up to desk, followed by* MARY *to his* R.*)* I'll tell you what we'll do! *(Presses a buzzer)* We carried forty-eight States in the campaign, didn't we? Mary and I?

FULTON. Yeah.

WINTERGREEN. And there was Devereaux propaganda then. But we licked it before. and we can do it again.

JENKINS. *(Enters L.)* Yes, sir.

WINTERGREEN. Those newspaper men still out there?

JENKINS. Yes, sir.

WINTERGREEN. Bring 'em in when I ring.

JENKINS. Yes, sir. *(Exits L.)*

WINTERGREEN. The trouble with you boys is you're yellow.

FULTON. Now, look here!

WINTERGREEN. One sock and you're ready to quit. We've got to fight, that's all. I'm as good as I ever was. And so's Mary. And we still love each other. *(Turning to her)* Don't we?

MARY. *(With spirit)* You bet we do.

WINTERGREEN. *(Swinging back onto the* MEN*)* There you are! We're not through. We haven't begun to fight. By God, we can tour again if we have to. I can still sing. Once a trouper, always a trouper. (MARY *is freshening the lipstick through all this.)* What do you say, boys? Are you with me?

ALL. Yes. (WINTERGREEN *presses the buzzer.)*

FULTON. You got to put it over, Jack.

WINTERGREEN. I'll put it over. I'll give them the best performance since Richard Mansfield. Are you ready, Mary?

MARY. *(Finishing the makeup job)* Ready!

WINTERGREEN. *(As a* SECRETARY *enters)* Bring in those damn newspaper men. (JONES *and* LYONS *cross behind desk to* GILHOOLEY *and* LIPPMAN. *MUSIC strikes up. Enter* 12 NEWSPAPER MEN L.*)*

WINTERGREEN. Well, gentlemen, what's on your mind?

REPORTERS.

We don't want to know about the moratorium,
Or how near we are to beer,
Or about the League of Nations,
Or the seventeen vacations,
You have had since you've been here.
Here's the one thing that the people of America
Are beside themselves to know:
They would like to know what's doing
On the lady who is suing
You—Diana Devereaux?
Ev'rybody wants to know:
What about Miss Devereaux?
From the highest to the low:
What about Miss Devereaux?

WINTERGREEN.

It's a pleasant day—
That's all I can say!

MARY.
 Here's the one thing we'll announce:
 Love's the only thing that counts!
REPORTERS.
 People want to know:
 What of Devereaux?
WINTERGREEN.
 When the one you love is near
 Nothing else can interfere.
ALL.
 When the one you love is near
 Nothing else can interfere.
WINTERGREEN.
 Here's some information
 I will gladly give the nation:
 I am for the true love;
 Here's the only girl I do love.
MARY.
 I love him and he loves me,
 And that's how it will always be,
 So what care we about Miss Devereaux?
BOTH.
 Who cares what the public chatters,
 Love's the only thing that matters.
WINTERGREEN.
 Who cares
 If the sky cares to fall in the sea?
 Who cares what banks fail in Yonkers—
 Long as you've got a kiss that conquers.
 Why should I care?
 Life is one long jubilee,
 So long as I care for you
 And you care for me.

(ALL *repeat Chorus twice,* WINTERGREEN *and* MARY *dancing.*
 REPORTERS *exit* L. *at end of second Chorus. As* REPORTERS
 leave, there is a Chorus of approval from the COMMITTEE.)

WINTERGREEN. Nothing at all, boys! I owe it all to the little
woman.
 MARY. You were grand, John.
 FULTON. I never heard you in better voice.
 WINTERGREEN. Did you hear that F sharp I gave them?
 GILHOOLEY. Great!
 WINTERGREEN. *(Letting his voice loose for a second in a*

snatch of operatic aria) Do you know what I'll do? I'll go on the radio every night! Mary and I!

FULTON. National Biscuit Company! They've been after you.

JONES. National Biscuit! That's a very popular hour in the West.

WINTERGREEN. A new song every night! I'll even get a megaphone.

MARY. And we can make records.

WINTERGREEN. They don't sell any more.

FULTON. Well, every little helps.

MARY. And I can still bake.

WINTERGREEN. What!

MARY. Corn muffins! Corn muffins for the unemployed!

WINTERGREEN. That's my girl. You feed 'em and I'll sing to them. We'll get the country back. Give us a week and they'll forget that Devereaux ever lived. *(A chorus of approval from the* COMMITTEE.) And you fellows wanted to quit! Why, we haven't begun to fight! This is a cinch! What would you do if a real fight came alone! *(Four bars of "Garcon, s'il vous plait" from the orchestra.* 6 GIRL SECRETARIES *enter* L., *line up along* L. *wall, downstage.)* What's this?

GIRL SECRETARIES. The French Ambassador!

WINTERGREEN. I can't see him! *(Four bars of "Garcon" repeated as* 6 BOY SECRETARIES *enter* L., *line up across stage.)* And what's this?

BOY SECRETARIES. The French Ambassador!

WINTERGREEN. I can't see him! (6 FRENCH SOLDIERS *enter* L., *march downstage in exaggerated goose-step.)* And what's this? (FRENCH SOLDIERS *go into song.)*

SOLDIERS.

> Garcon, s'il vous plait,
> Encore Chevrolet Coupe;
> Papah, pooh, pooh, pooh!
> A vous toot dir veh, a vous?
> Garcon, q'est-ce que c'est?
> Tra la, Maurice Chevalier!
> J'adore crepes Suzette
> Et aussi Lafayette!

And now we give the meaning of this song:

We're six of the fifty million and we can't be wrong!

SECRETARIES.

They're six of the fifty million and they can't be wrong.

(FRENCH AMBASSADOR *enters* L.)

FRENCH SOLDIERS. Ze French Ambassador!

WINTERGREEN. I still can't see him.

FRENCH AMBASSADOR. I am the Ambassador of France—

WINTERGREEN. Europe?

FRENCH AMBASSADOR. And I have come to see a grievous wrong righted. My country is deeply hurt. Not since the days of Louis the Seventh, the Eighth, the Ninth, the Tenth, and possibly the Eleventh has such a thing happened!

WINTERGREEN. What's troubling you?

FRENCH AMBASSADOR. You have done a great injustice to a French descendant—a lovely girl, whose rights have been trampled in the dust!

WINTERGREEN, MARY and COMMITTEE. Who is she? What's her name?

FRENCH AMBASSADOR. Her name is Diana Devereaux.

WINTERGREEN, MARY and COMMITTEE. Diana Devereaux! Diana Devereaux! Since when is she of French descent?

FRENCH AMBASSADOR.
> I've been looking up her family tree
> And I have found a most important pedigree!
> She's the illegitimate daughter of an illegitimate son—
> Of an illegitimate nephew of Napoleon!

ALL. *(Awed)* Napoleon!

FRENCH AMBASSADOR.
> She offers aristocracy
> To this bizarre democracy
> Where naught is sacred but the old simoleon!
> I must know why
> You crucify
> My native country
> With this effront'ry
> To the illegitimate daughter of an illegitimate son
> Of an illegitimate nephew of Napoleon!

ALL.
> To the illegitimate daughter of an illegitimate son
> Of an illegitimate nephew of Napoleon!

ALL. *(To WINTERGREEN)*
> You so-and-so!
> We didn't know
> She had a tie-up
> So very high up.
> She's the illegitimate daughter of an illegitimate son
> Of an illegitimate nephew of Napoleon!

DIANA. *(Off L.)* Oh— *(Enters)* I was the most beautiful blossom in all the Southland. I—

MARY and WINTERGREEN. We know all that.

FRENCH AMBASSADOR. You know all that—but you *don't* know the misery of this poor little girl who has suffered because—

COMMITTEE. Because—?

MARY *and* WINTERGREEN. Because—?

FRENCH AMBASSADOR. Because— *(Motioning to* DIANA *to go ahead.)*

DIANA.

    Because, because, because, because
    I won the competition
    But I got no recognition,
    And because he broke my heart!
      (Indicating WINTERGREEN.)
    Because, because, because, because
    The man who ought to love me
    Tried to make a monkey of me;
    Double-crossing from the start!
    I might have been First Lady,
    But now my past is shady—
    Oh, pity this poor maidie!

FRENCH AMBASSADOR *and* DIANA.

    And there's the man who ought to pay!

ALL.

    Because, because, because, because
    She won the prize for beauty
    And he didn't do his duty
    He has broken her poor heart!

FRENCH AMBASSADOR. *(To* WINTERGREEN) You see how this poor child has suffered. And so, on behalf of France, I demand that your marriage be annulled and that you marry Diana.

WINTERGREEN. Never! Never!

FRENCH AMBASSADOR. Then you will arouse the anger of France and you must be prepared to face the consequences.

(SOLDIERS *line up with* AMBASSADOR *and* DIANA. *They march off* L., *singing first four lines, "Garcon, s'il vous plait.")*

FULTON. Jack, you've got to do something about this.

WINTERGREEN. Leave Mary? Never!

FULTON.

    We are all in this together;
    We are birdies of a feather;
    And if you don't change your thesis
    Then our party goes to pieces!

LYONS.
All our jobs you'll be destroying
With your attitude annoying.
GILHOOLEY.
You will get us all in trouble!
And in spades, sir, which is double!
WINTERGREEN.
I will never leave my Mary!
LYONS.
Since he's acting so contrary
Send him off on a vacation!
GILHOOLEY.
I suggest his resignation!
    (LYONS *back to place.*)
WINTERGREEN.
Resignation?
ALL.
Resignation!
FULTON. *(Coming to him)*
You've got to face it—this is a crisis!
To leave your Mary you may decline,
But to save us, my good advice is
You resign!
    (Back to place.)
ALL.   *(WARN Draw Curtain.)*
Yes, resign!
WINTERGREEN.
I assure you—though it's a crisis,
To leave my Mary I must decline,
And I don't care what your advice is,
I decline to resign!
MARY.
We decline to resign!
COMMITTEE. *(To each other)*
He is stubborn—we must teach him;
I'm afraid we must impeach him!
ALL.
He is stubborn—we must teach him;
He has forced us to impeach him!
You decline to resign,
    (They start backing out in tempo)
So we'll teach you!
We'll impeach you!
    (ALL *start to exit*)
You decline to resign,
We don't envy you at all!

You decline to resign,
So we'll teach you,
We'll impeach you!
   (COMMITTEE *off* R. OTHERS L.)
You decline to resign—
Humpty Dumpty has to fall!
   (And off.)

(LIGHTS Dim—Arcs and Stage.)

WINTERGREEN *and* MARY.
Who cares
If the sky cares to fall in the sea?
WINTERGREEN.
We two together can win out.
Just remember to stick your chin out.

(ARC SPOT Dim.)
(Start Draw Curtain.)

MARY.
Why should we care?
Life is one long jubilee—
BOTH.
So long as I care for you
And you care for me!

BLACKOUT. DRAW CURTAIN CLOSED.

ACT TWO

SCENE II

STAGE LIGHTS up. Open Draw Curtain.

SCENE: *The scene is a corridor in the Capitol, immediately
outside the Senate. The doors to the Senate are at C.—
two swinging doors, not unlike those found in our more ele-
gant movie palaces. In neat letters above the doors are
the words: "UNITED STATES SENATE."*

AT RISE: A PAGE *enters* L.; *goes through the doors* C.
   Immediately the Committee, FULTON, GILHOOLEY,
LYONS, JONES *and* LIPPMAN, *enter* R., *talking as they
enter.*

FULTON. Say, I'm just as sorry as anybody. I like Jack as
much as you do, and I'd give my shirt not to have to do this.

JONES. We can't be sentimental at a time like this.
GILHOOLEY. Say! Wait a minute!
FULTON. Yah!

(THROTTLEBOTTOM *enters* L., *just as he had left the White House.)*

GILHOOLEY. If he's put out of office who becomes the President?
JONES. Why, the Vice President, of course.
FULTON. *(As it dawns on him)* We haven't got a Vice President.
GILHOOLEY. Sure we have! He came up to the room.
FULTON. *(Suddenly remembering)* Pitts! I nominated him.

(A chorus of dissent. LIPPMAN : *"No, that wasn't his name!"* JONES: *"It was Schaeffer!"* LYONS: *"No, not Pitts!"* GILHOOLEY: *"No, it was a longer name—Barbinelli!")*

THROTTLEBOTTOM. *(Who has been listening to all this in full expectation of imminent discovery, now comes over to them)* Hello, gentlemen! *(In a knot, the other* FIVE *continue the argument, repeating their original statements.)*
FULTON. It was Alexander Something.
GILHOOLEY. Yah, that's it!
THROTTLEBOTTOM. Throttlebottom.
GILHOOLEY. That's right! *(A chorus from the* OTHERS: *"Yes, that's right!" "What's his name?")*
FULTON. *(Realizing that it is a stranger who has spoken)* Oh! Thank you. *(Hands him a cigar.)*
THROTTLEBOTTOM. Oh, thank you, Mr. Fulton.
FULTON. *(Looking at him)* Haven't I seen you before some place?
THROTTLEBOTTOM. I'm Throttlebottom.
FULTON. Huh?
THROTTLEBOTTOM. Throttlebottom. The Vice President. That's how I knew the name. *(A chorus of greetings. "Well, hello!" "Where have you been?" "Well, for God's sake!" "Here! Have a light!")*
FULTON. Well, for heaven's sake! Just the fellow we were looking for!
GILHOOLEY. Yes, sir!
FULTON. We want to talk to you!
THROTTLEBOTTOM. Me?
LYONS. That's what!
FULTON. We've got a surprise for you!

THROTTLEBOTTOM. *(Covering his eyes)* A surprise?

LIPPMAN. Sure! Remember I told you you had a chance to be President?

THROTTLEBOTTOM. Yeah!

FULTON. Well, we've been thinking it over and we're going to make you President!

GILHOOLEY. That's what we are!

THROTTLEBOTTOM. President! Say! You mean of the United States?

JONES. That's what we do!

THROTTLEBOTTOM. But what was the matter with the othei fellow?

FULTON. We're going to impeach him!

GILHOOLEY. He wouldn't play ball with us.

THROTTLEBOTTOM. Well, I don't play very good— *(Ad lib. start out—voice from* ALL.)

FULTON. Come on! Let's get started! *(Starting for the C. door.)*

GILHOOLEY. Yeah, we've got work to do!

THROTTLEBOTTOM. You really mean it? I'm not Vice President any more?

JONES. Not if we impeach the President! *(Starts for C. door.)*

THROTTLEBOTTOM. Well, when do we do that?

JONES. Right now! Come on!

FULTON. You've got to preside over the Senate. (LIPPMAN, FULTON *and* GILHOOLEY *exit* C.)

THROTTLEBOTTOM. And after that I'll be President?

LYONS. That's what you will! (LYONS *and* JONES *exit* C. SCRUBWOMAN *enters* L.)

THROTTLEBOTTOM. President! Say! How will that sound? President Alexander Bottlethrottom. *(Corrects himself)* Throttlebottom.

SCRUBWOMAN. Huh?

THROTTLEBOTTOM. *(He dances up to her)* I'm going to be President!

SCRUBWOMAN. I'd rather have this job. It's steady. *(Exits* R. *Enter* WINTERGREEN *and* JENKINS L.)

JENKINS. Well, it's a dirty trick, Chief. That's all I've got to say.

WINTERGREEN. Well, it's politics. They've got to eat, too.

JENKINS. Want me to go in with you?

WINTERGREEN. No. I want to handle this alone.

JENKINS. More power to you, Chief. *(Takes his hand; holds it during following speech)* And I want you to know that, if the worst comes to the worst, and they fire you out—

WINTERGREEN. I know—if they fire me out you want a job with the next President.

JENKINS. Right! *(Exits* L. WINTERGREEN *starts for* C. *door.)*

THROTTLEBOTTOM. *(Who has been standing* R.*)* Hello, Mr. President.

WINTERGREEN. *(Not recognizing* THROTTLEBOTTOM*)* How do you do?

THROTTLEBOTTOM. I'll bet you don't remember me, do you?

WINTERGREEN. *(After a moment's thought)* You're the fellow that gave me that dill pickle.

THROTTLEBOTTOM. That's right.

WINTERGREEN. What are you doing now?

THROTTLEBOTTOM. I'm Vice President.

WINTERGREEN. You don't say? Lost your other job, huh?

THROTTLEBOTTOM. Well, I'm going to have a good job now, because I'm going to be President.

WINTERGREEN. *(Realizing it)* Say, that's right! If they kick me out that makes you President. *(Looks at him)* The country certainly *is* in a hole.

THROTTLEBOTTOM. Say, I wonder if you'd mind doing me a favor?

WINTERGREEN. Sure!

THROTTLEBOTTOM. You see, I don't know anything about being President. I just found out today how to be Vice President.

WINTERGREEN. Well, that's something.

THROTTLEBOTTOM. Isn't there some book I could read?

WINTERGREEN. Sure—I'm writing one. *"What Every Young President Ought To Know."*

THROTTLEBOTTOM. Has it got pictures?

WINTERGREEN. It's got everything. Tells you just what to do. Of course the first four years are easy. You don't do anything except try to get re-elected.

THROTTLEBOTTOM. That's pretty hard these days.

WINTERGREEN. The next four years you wonder why the hell you wanted to be re-elected. Then you go fishing.

THROTTLEBOTTOM. Well, couldn't I save a lot of time and go fishing right now?

WINTERGREEN. No, you got to wait until an important matter comes up and then you go fishing.

THROTTLEBOTTOM. Well, do you ever catch any fish?

WINTERGREEN. Well, I'm the President.

(WARN BLACKOUT and Draw Curtains.)

THROTTLEBOTTOM. Yeah, but it's a pretty hard job being President. You've got to keep on writing those Thanksgiving proclamations, no matter what—and then there's that other bunch, Congress— I guess there isn't anything you can really do about Congress, is there?

WINTERGREEN. Well, you could keep them out of Washington.

THROTTLEBOTTOM. Can you do that?

WINTERGREEN. Saint Patrick did it—keep them out—quarantine the place. Get the measles.

THROTTLEBOTTOM. I had measles once.

WINTERGREEN. Yeah, but you never had Congress. That's worse.

THROTTLEBOTTOM. Oh! What about those messages that the President is always sending to Congress—who reads those, anyway?

WINTERGREEN. The fellow who prints 'em.

THROTTLEBOTTOM. Well, wouldn't everybody read them if you made 'em funnier?

WINTERGREEN. Some of them have been pretty funny.

THROTTLEBOTTOM. Couldn't you make a speech instead? Then they'd have to listen.

WINTERGREEN. No, no! You've got to be careful about speeches. You only make a speech when you want the stock market to go down.

THROTTLEBOTTOM. What do you do when you want the stock market to go up?

WINTERGREEN. Oh, boy! wouldn't I like to know! *(A big handshake.)*

BLACKOUT.

DRAW CURTAINS CLOSE.

ACT TWO

SCENE III

Stage LIGHTS up. On the bass trill of the introduction to the song, the curtains open.

SCENE: *The Senate Chamber. In the C. of the R. wall is a platform about five feet high, on which are the desk and chair of the presiding officer. The desk is reached by two stairs, one upstage and one down, both curving into the room. The senatorial desks are set in a semi-circle at stage L., facing the platform, in three rows, the last of which*

is partly offstage. There are chairs for eighteen SENA-
TORS. *In the back wall,* C., *are large double doors. They
are up on a platform three steps high.*

AT RISE: THROTTLEBOTTOM, *the* CHIEF CLERK, *and the* SENA-
TORS, *most of them heavily bearded, are in their places.
They are humming and swaying back and forth rhyth-
mically.*

(At rise ALL *the* SENATORS *are humming and swaying to tune.)*

THROTTLEBOTTOM. The Senator from North Dakota?
SENATOR. Present!
THROTTLEBOTTOM. Check! The Senator from Minnesota?
SENATOR. Present!
THROTTLEBOTTOM. Check! The Senator from Lou'siana?
LYONS. Present!
THROTTLEBOTTOM. Check! The Senator who's from Mon-
tana?
SENATOR. Present!
THROTTLEBOTTOM. Check! The Senator who's from Alaska?
SENATOR. Present!
THROTTLEBOTTOM. Check! The Senator who's from Ne-
braska?
SENATOR. Present!
THROTTLEBOTTOM. Check!
    The Senators from other states will have to bide their time,
    For I simply can't be bothered when the names don't
        rhyme!
ALL.
    He simply can't be bothered when the names don't rhyme.
    The Senators from other states will have to bide their time,
    For he simply can't be bothered when the names don't
        rhyme!
ALL. Ha ha ha ha ha ha ha ha ha ha ha ha ha!
        (All the SENATORS *fall sound asleep.)*
CLERK. *(At finish of the number)* It is now twelve o'clock
noon and the Senate of the United States is hereby declared in
session. *(Hands gavel up to* THROTTLEBOTTOM.*)*
THROTTLEBOTTOM. Gentlemen, when you hear the musical
note it will be exactly twelve o'clock noon. *(Brings gavel down
with a resounding bang. It lands right on the watch which he
has just taken from his pocket and laid on the desk, completely
splintering it. Shakes the watch, then puts it back in his
pocket. The* SENATORS *are awakened by the gavel.)* Well, gentlemen, I'm glad to meet you all. You'll have to excuse me for

not knowing much about this job. I see I made one mistake already—I went and got shaved. Now let's get at things. I'm only going to be with you one day, so let's make it a pip. Now what have we got to take up?

CLERK. *(Announcing)* The first thing before the Senate is unfinished business.

THROTTLEBOTTOM. Unfinished business—is that still going on? But aren't we going to impeach the President?

CLERK. That comes later. *(Announcing)* Unfinished business!

SENATOR FROM MASSACHUSETTS. *(Rises)* Mr. Chairman! Mr. Chairman!

CLERK. *(To* THROTTLEBOTTOM*)* That's you.

THROTTLEBOTTOM. Oh, I thought I was just Vice President.

CLERK. You must recognize the Senator from Massachusetts. (SENATOR *crosses* C.*)*

THROTTLEBOTTOM. Oh, hello! How's everything in Massachusetts?

SENATOR FROM MASSACHUSETTS. Mr. Chairman! I rise to protest against a great injustice! In Seventeen Hundred and Seventy-Five Paul Revere made the famous ride that saved this country from the greedy clutch of England.

THROTTLEBOTTOM. That's right—I read about that. "Listen, my children—" *(Informally, to the* CLERK*)* He went from one house to another, and he knocked on the door, but by the time they came out he was at the next house. *(A glare from the* SENATOR*)* Well, you want to make anything out of it?

SENATOR FROM MASSACHUSETTS. Because of this great exploit, Paul Revere's name has been given the affectionate tribute of a great people. But what of that gallant figure who is even more responsible? Gentlemen, what about Jenny, Paul Revere's horse? *(Applause.)* Surely, gentlemen, Jenny is entitled to the protection of a governmental pension. A bill providing such a pension was introduced into this body in the year Eighteen Hundred and Four, and came up for its first reading in Eighteen Hundred and Fifty-Two.

THROTTLEBOTTOM. I wasn't here then. That fellow there might know something about it. *(Pointing to bearded* SENATOR.*)*

SENATOR FROM MASSACHUSETTS. Gentlemen, in these hundred and forty-five years Jenny has not been getting any younger. I ask you, gentlemen, what are we going to do about Jenny?

THROTTLEBOTTOM. Well, that's unfinished business if I ever heard it.

JONES. May I point out to the Senator from Massachusetts that Jenny is dead?

THROTTLEBOTTOM. She is? What do you think of that? Good old Jenny! When did she die?

JONES. She died in Eighteen Hundred and Five.

THROTTLEBOTTOM. The Senate will rise for one minute in silent tribute to the departed horse from Massachusetts. *(They rise. He bangs the gavel)* Well, that finishes Jenny. *(The* SENATOR *angrily returns to his seat.)* Is there any other unfinished business?

LYONS. *(Crosses* C.*)* Mr. Chairman! Gentlemen! I crave the indulgence of this august body while I say a few words in honor of my wife's birthday. *(Applause.)* And I move you, Mr. Chairman, that the Senate appropriate five thousand dollars for flowers to be sent her on this historic occasion.

SENATOR FROM NORTH DAKOTA. Second the motion!

THROTTLEBOTTOM. All in favor say "Aye"! *(A full-throated "Aye" from the assemblage.)* Motion carried! *(To the* CLERK*)* Put in my card. (LYONS *indignantly goes to his chair and sits.)*

THROTTLEBOTTOM. Now, what comes next? How about impeaching the President?

CLERK. *(Handing him a sheet of paper)* Mr. Vice President—

THROTTLEBOTTOM. What's this?

CLERK. *(Indicating the paper)* The following committees are ready to report.

THROTTLEBOTTOM. *(Consulting the paper)* Oh, what a lot of committees! I don't know which— *(Closes his eyes, one finger suspended over the paper)* Eenie, meenie, minie, mo. Catch a committee by the toe. If they holler give 'em dough; eenie, meenie, minie, mo. *(Places his finger on the paper; looks to see what committee he has selected. Announces)* Committee on Unemployment.

JONES. *(Rising)* The Committee on Unemployment is gratified to report that due to its unremitting efforts there is now more unemployment in the United States than ever before. *(Sits.)*

THROTTLEBOTTOM. Now we're getting some place. Now let's impeach the President.

SENATOR FROM MASSACHUSETTS. *(Rising)* Mr. Chairman: I would like to call the attention of the Senate to a matter that has been puzzling me for some time. It has to do with a very interesting bridge hand, in which the cards were distributed as follows: East held the four aces, West the four kings, North the four queens, and South—ah—nothing of any importance.

LYONS. *(Rising indignantly)* Mr. Chairman! *(Faces the* SENATOR FROM MASSACHUSETTS*)* The South will never stand for a hand like that! *(After a glare they* BOTH *sit.)*

CLERK. *(Recitative)* The next business before the Senate is the resolution on the impeachment of the President.

(A FANFARE of trumpets. TWO PAGES *enter up* C., *take their places at either side of* C. *door.)*

PAGES. *(Announcing)* The President of the United States!

THROTTLEBOTTOM. Who?

CLERK. The President of the United States! (WINTERGREEN *enters* C.; *comes down to below* THROTTLEBOTTOM'S *desk.)*

THROTTLEBOTTOM. Oh, Mr. President, won't you sit down while we kick you out? (WINTERGREEN *sits in chair* R. *under rostrum. Enter* FULTON, LIPPMAN, GILHOOLEY C. *They come to* C. *and are joined by* LYONS.*)*

FULTON, LIPPMAN, GILHOOLEY. *(A quartet)* Whereas—

LYONS. *(As others close eyes)* At a meeting of the Senate at which a quorum was present a motion was made and it was proposed that—

SENATORS. Whereas—

LYONS. John P. Wintergreen has undertaken to marry the winner of a contest held at Atlantic City—

SENATORS. Whereas—

LYONS. His subsequent refusal to marry the winner, Miss Diana Devereaux, will lead to dire international complications—

SENATORS. Whereas—

LYONS. Now, therefore, be it resolved that President John P. Wintergreen be, and he hereby is, impeached from the said office of President of these United States.

JONES. I second the resolution. (GILHOOLEY *and* LIPPMAN *to back of rostrum.)*

FULTON. Our first witness—the French Ambassador. (FULTON *to back of rostrum.)*

(Enter C. *the* 6 FRENCH SOLDIERS *as in Act II, Scene I, to* C.*)*

FRENCH SOLDIERS.

> Garcon, s'il vous plait,
> Encore, Chevrolet Coupe;
> Papah, pooh, pooh, pooh!
> A vous toot dir vay a vous?

SENATORS.

> We say how de do,
> Which means that we welcome you;
> We're glad of the chance
> To say hello to France.

(FRENCH SOLDIERS *march upstage as* FRENCH AMBASSADOR
enters c.)

FRENCH AMBASSADOR.

> You've dealt a lovely maid
> A blow that is injurious;
> A very dirty trick was played,
> And France is simply furious!

SENATORS.

> He says a lovely maid
> Was dealt a blow injurious;
> He says a dirty trick was played,
> And France is simply furious.

FULTON. *(To* AMBASSADOR*)* Ambassador, please explain
why France should be concerned about the plaintiff. (FULTON
back to position.)

FRENCH AMBASSADOR.

> She's the illegitimate daughter of an illegitimate son
> Of an illegitimate nephew of Napoleon!

ALL. Napoleon!

FRENCH AMBASSADOR.

> She's contemplating suicide
> Because that man he threw aside
> A lady with the blue blood of Napoleon.
> What sort of man
> Is this who can
> Insult my country
> With this effront'ry?

ALL.

> To the illegitimate daughter of an illegitimate son
> Of an illegitimate nephew of Napoleon!

FRENCH AMBASSADOR. The Atlantic City witnesses—(8
SHOWGIRLS, *in white bathing suits, with red, white and blue
scarves, march on* c.*)*—and Miss Diana Devereaux. (DIANA
enters c.)

DIANA. I have come all ze way from France to bring ze
greetings. (WINTERGREEN *rises and goes down* R.*)*

FRENCH AMBASSADOR. Tell your story, little one. Com-
mencez, s'il vous plait. (GIRLS *close in semi-circle behind her.)*

DIANA. (ALL *swaying*)
>Jilted, jilted,
>I'm a flow'r that's wilted;
>Blighted, blighted,
>Till the wrong is righted;
>Broken, broken,
>By a man soft-spoken;
>Faded, faded,
>Heaven knows why.
>When men are deceivers, I'm afraid
>'Tis sad to be a trusting maid.
>Jilted, jilted, jilted am I,
>Oh, what is there left but to die?

(GIRLS *walk* R. *to below rostrum in two lines of four.)*

ALL.
>Jilted, jilted,
>She's a flow'r that's wilted!
>Blighted, blighted,
>Till the wrong is righted;
>Broken, broken,
>By a man soft-spoken;
>Faded, faded,
>Heaven knows why.

DIANA.
Just as in the Frankie and Johnny song,
THROTTLEBOTTOM.
He done her wrong!
ALL.
He done her wrong!
>Jilted, jilted, jilted is she,
>Oh, what is there left but—to dee?
>Boo-hoo, boo-hoo, boo-hoo-o-o-o.

(FRENCH AMBASSADOR *and* DIANA *over* L.C. SENATE *is visibly affected;* ALL *are crying into handkerchiefs.)*

THROTTLEBOTTOM. And, now, Mr. President, what have you to say for yourself?
WINTERGREEN. *(Up to* C. *below rostrum)*
Impeach me! Fine me! Jail me! Sue me!
My Mary's love means much more to me!
THROTTLEBOTTOM.
Enough, enough! We want no preachment!
It's time to vote on his impeachment!

ALL. (SENATORS *sit)*
    It's time to vote on his impeachment!
THROTTLEBOTTOM.
    The Senator from Minnesota?
SENATOR.
    Guilty!
THROTTLEBOTTOM.
    Check! The Senator from North Dakota?
SENATOR.
    Guilty!
THROTTLEBOTTOM.
    Check! The Senator from Lou'siana?
SENATOR.
    Guilty!
THROTTLEBOTTOM.
    Check! The Senator who's from Montana?
MARY. *(Breaks into room from* C. *Comes down* C. *Recitative)* Stop! Stop! Stop!
WINTERGREEN. Mary!
MARY.
    Before you go any further—with your permission,
    I must tell you of my husband's delicate condition.

(FULTON, GILHOOLEY *and* LYONS *move downstage behind her.)*

ALL.
    Delicate condition! What do you mean?
MARY.
            I'm about to be a mother;
            He's about to be a father; (ALL *register.)*
            We're about to have a baby;

(WINTERGREEN *is congratulated by the* COMMITTEE.*)*

            I must tell it,
            These doings compel it!
            Oh, I'm about to be a mother;
            He's about to be a father;
            We're about to have a baby.

(WINTERGREEN *does proud father business.)*

ALL.
            A baby!

MARY.
            A baby to love and adore—
            Who could ask for anything more?

ALL.

> She's about to be a mother;
> He's about to be a father;
> They're about to have a baby.
> We can't bother
> A budding young father!

(MUSIC continues; SENATORS *swaying in time.* MARY *is pirouetting in a dance. The* SENATOR FROM MASSACHUSETTS *is doing a cartwheel; all the* SENATORS *are dancing joyously.)*

WINTERGREEN. *(Near* CLERK*)* Mary, is it true? Am I to have a baby?

MARY. *(Over* L.C., *coming half to him)* It's true, John; it's true.

WINTERGREEN. It's wonderful, it's wonderful—water!—water! *(Faints.* CLERK *catches him. A laugh and a cheer from* SENATORS. MARY *at his side.)*

ALL. *(Picking up song again)*
> They're about to have a baby—a baby—

DIANA. *(Breaking in)* It eez a fine countree—I am compromised and she has ze babee!

THROTTLEBOTTOM. Gentlemen, gentlemen—this country has never yet impeached an expectant father. What do you say?

SENATORS. Not guilty!

THROTTLEBOTTOM. *(To* WINTERGREEN*)* You can still be President and I'll go back to Vice!

FRENCH AMBASSADOR. *(Crossing down to* WINTERGREEN*)*
> Sacre! I go to the telegraph office to cable my report;
> This is American trickery of the most reprehensible sort!

(Starts to exit, crossing down toward L.; *stopped by* DIANA's *singing.)*

DIANA.
> I was the most beautiful blossom—

*(*FRENCH AMBASSADOR *takes her by the hand; leads her off* L.I.*)*

> —in all the Southland.

GIRLS.
> Strike up the cymbals, drum and fife, *(Start to exit* R.I*)*
> One of us was to be the President's wife.

SENATOR FROM MASSACHUSETTS. Great work, Jack; you'll be reinstated in the hearts of the American people.

JONES. You're doing your duty by posterity.

WINTERGREEN. Posterity? Why, posterity is just around the corner. (SENATORS *and* COMMITTEE *come downstage, surrounding* WINTERGREEN *and* MARY.)

(*WARN Blackout and Draw Curtains.*)

WINTERGREEN.

Posterity is just around the corner;

(SENATORS *bring out tambourines.*)

ALL.

Posterity is just around the corner!

MARY.

It really doesn't pay to be a mourner.

ALL.

Posterity is just around the corner!

WINTERGREEN.

Posterity is here—I don't mean maybe!

ALL.

There's nothing guarantees it like a baby!

MARY.

Posterity is here and will continue!

ALL.

We really didn't know you had it in you!
Posterity
Is in its infancy!

WINTERGREEN.

I sing to ev'ry citizen and fore'gner:

ALL.

Posterity is just around the corner!

(THROTTLEBOTTOM, *with a bass drum, is leading a march around the stage, followed by* MARY, *dancing, and* WINTERGREEN, *borne on the shoulders of two of the* SENATORS. *The drum bears the legend "Wintergreen for President," but the "Wintergreen" is crossed out and "Throttlebottom" is substituted.*)

ALL.

We'll soon be pulling plums, like Jackie Horner!
Posterity is just around the—
Oomp-osterity, oomp-osterity, oompah, oompah, oomp-osterity.

Oomp-osterity, oomp-osterity, oompah, oompah, oomp-osterity is just around the corner!
Around the corner!

(Third beat of "corner")

BLACKOUT. DRAW CURTAINS.

ACT TWO

SCENE IV

STAGE LIGHTS Up. Open Draw Curtains.

SCENE: *In one—a corridor in the White House.*

Enter JENKINS *and* MISS BENSON L. *They are singing "Posterity" as they come on.*

JENKINS. It'll certainly be great to have a baby in the White House. I wonder when it'll be born.

MISS BENSON. Let's see—they were married March fourth, weren't they?

JENKINS. That's right.

MISS BENSON. *(Counting on her fingers)* April, May, June, July, August, September, October, November, *December!* It'll be born in December.

JENKINS. How do you know?

MISS BENSON. Well, it won't be born *before* December.

JENKINS. How do you know?

MISS BENSON. Oh, the President wouldn't do a thing like that. He'd never be re-elected.

JENKINS. You can't tell. Might be the very thing that would re-elect him. What a platform!

MISS BENSON. It's certainly wonderful the way this has lined people up behind the President.

JENKINS. Yeah, but we don't know what France is going to do. She's still liable to make trouble.

MISS BENSON My, you'd think a woman could have a baby without France butting in.

JENKINS. Well, fifty million Frenchmen—they've got to do something.

MISS BENSON. Let 'em do it in Paris. Why should they come over here and—

WINTERGREEN. *(Singing as he enters* R.*)* "Somebody's coming to our house; somebody's coming to stay—" Oh, hello.

JENKINS. Hi, Chief!

MISS BENSON. Good morning, Mr. President. And how is Mrs. Wintergreen this morning?

WINTERGREEN. *(Vaguely)* Who? Mrs. Wintergreen? *(Realizes that there is such a person)* Oh, she's fine! Fine! Yes, sir! *(Tapping his own chest)* Should have seen the breakfast I ate!

MISS BENSON. Tell me, Mr. President. Ah—*(Hesitantly)* —when is the baby expected?

WINTERGREEN. Well, of course, you can't tell about such things, but we think some time in November. *(*JENKINS *gives* BENSON *a slap that says, "What did I tell you?"* WINTERGREEN *catches it, does some quick counting on his fingers, corrects himself)* December.

MISS BENSON. *(Slaps* JENKINS *in triumph)* Oh, December.

WINTERGREEN. Yes, we sort of thought December would be a very nice month. End the old year right and all that sort of thing. Have a cigar? Oh, pardon me, the baby isn't born yet.

FULTON. *(Enters* R.*)* Hello, Jack!

WINTERGREEN. Hello, there! Should have seen the breakfast I ate. *(To the* SECRETARIES*)* See you later.

MISS BENSON. *(To* JENKINS*)* I told you December.

JENKINS. Yeah—well, I'd still like to make a bet on it. *(He and* BENSON *exit* R.*)*

FULTON. Well, Jack, how are you? And how's the wife?

WINTERGREEN. Fine, fine! Never felt better.

FULTON. Mighty smart girl, Mary. She certainly saved the day for us.

WINTERGREEN. *She* saved the day? I suppose I was just an innocent bystander?

FULTON. I don't mean that, but I thought it sort of came as a surprise to you.

WINTERGREEN. Surprise? Why, I planned the whole thing. I foresaw the situation months ago.

FULTON. Anyway, it settled France. They're still yelling, but there's nothing they can do about it. The American people are behind you to a man. How'd you ever get the idea, Jack?

WINTERGREEN. Why, it wasn't anything. Nothing at all. Anybody in my place would have done the same.

FULTON. Yes, sir, it'll be a wonderful thing to have a baby in the White House.

WINTERGREEN. You mean instead of the President?

FULTON. No, no, Jack—I mean it. I tell you, there's some-

thing about the patter of baby feet, trickling down the stairs—
(Enter the FRENCH AMBASSADOR L.*)*

FRENCH AMBASSADOR. Gentlemen!

FULTON. *(With a bow)* Monsieur! *(To* WINTERGREEN*)* The French Ambassador.

FRENCH AMBASSADOR. *(With an elaborate bow)* Monsieur President.

WINTERGREEN. You all alone?

FRENCH AMBASSADOR. But yes.

WINTERGREEN. Where are those six guys with the trailing arbutus who used to march in ahead of you— *(His gesture carries out the idea of crossed bayonets, and even goes a bit further by bringing thumb and nose into close juxtaposition.)*

FRENCH AMBASSADOR. They could not come today. They have dancing lesson.

WINTERGREEN. You look kind of naked without them.

FRENCH AMBASSADOR. *(Acknowledges this with a bow)* You will pardon this intrusion, Monsieur, but I have received another note from my country.

WINTERGREEN. That's all right. We've got a lot of notes from your country, and some of them were due ten years ago.

FRENCH AMBASSADOR. But this is not a promise to pay—this is serious.

WINTERGREEN. O-oh!

FRENCH AMBASSADOR. *(Bows)* Monsieur, I have good news for you. France consents to your having the baby.

FULTON. Ah!

WINTERGREEN. France consents?

FRENCH AMBASSADOR. Freely.

WINTERGREEN. Why, that's wonderful of her. Good old France! Do you mind if I tell my wife, so she can go ahead? *(*AMBASSADOR *bows.)* You've no idea how this will please her. Will December be all right for France? *(Starts to go, then stops)* Won't take me a minute—I'll be right back.

FRENCH AMBASSADOR. But one moment, Monsieur. (WINTERGREEN *pauses.)* France consents, but on one condition.

WINTERGREEN. Yeah?

FRENCH AMBASSADOR. France must have the baby.

FULTON *and* WINTERGREEN. *What?*

FRENCH AMBASSADOR. Do not be hasty, Monsieur. You must understand the desperate situation of my country. For fifty years the birth-rate of France has been declining, declining, declining.

WINTERGREEN. What's that got to do with me?

FRENCH AMBASSADOR. You must see, Monsieur. If you had married Madamoiselle Devereaux, as you have promise, the baby she is French. But now you have taken away from France one baby, and she demand replacement.

(WARN Blackout.)

WINTERGREEN. Never!

FULTON. I should say not!

FRENCH AMBASSADOR. It is the old law, Monsieur; an eye for an eye, a tooth for a tooth, and a baby for a baby.

WINTERGREEN. You'll get no tooth from my baby.

FRENCH AMBASSADOR. The tooth, the whole tooth, and nothing but the tooth!

WINTERGREEN. Not one tooth!

FRENCH AMBASSADOR. That is your final word?

WINTERGREEN. It is! Good day, Monsieur!

FRENCH AMBASSADOR. Good day! *(Clicks his heels; salutes; turns and starts out)* Lafayette, we are coming! *(Exits L.)*

FULTON. What do you think France'll do?

WINTERGREEN. What's the worst she can do? Sue us for what she owes us?

FULTON. But that other thing! France is awful touchy about her birth-rate!

WINTERGREEN. What are you worrying about? I fixed *this* up, didn't I?

FULTON. What?

WINTERGREEN. Well, Mary's going to have a baby, isn't she?

FULTON. Yes!

WINTERGREEN. Well! Next year I make a tour of France! Lafayette! *(He salutes.)*

BLACKOUT.

DROP CURTAIN UP.

ACT TWO

SCENE V

STAGE and ARC LIGHTS Up.

SCENE: *The Yellow Room of the White House. A great crystal chandelier. A series of columns as far as the eye can see, giving the effect of an enormous ballroom. Entrances on each side.*

It is a magnificent room, and is made more so by the striking clothes of the WOMEN *and the uniforms of the*

MEN. *Those men who are not in full dress uniform wear evening clothes, with bands across their shirt fronts, and hung with medals and insignia.*

AT RISE: *The stage is almost filled—various groups are gathered together, chatting. Stretched across the stage, from one archway to the other, is a line of 4 gorgeously dressed* FLUNKEYS. GUESTS *are still arriving, and each one, as he enters, brings a baby carriage with him as a gift. The carriage is accepted by the* FIRST FLUNKEY *and is then passed down the line until it is shot off stage at the other side. When the Curtain rises each* FLUNKEY *is handing a baby carriage to the next one, and at the entrance new guests are bringing new carriages.*

As the FLUNKEYS *pass on the carriages they repeat the line that has been spoken as the gift arrived: "Compliments of Ecuador," "Compliments of Bolivia."*

There is an undercurrent of MUSIC throughout the scene.

CHIEF FLUNKEY. *(As another couple enter)* The Minister from Turkey!

MINISTER FROM TURKEY. *(Handing over baby carriage)* Compliments of Turkey. *(3* FLUNKEYS *repeat the line, as they do with the subsequent gifts.)*

CHIEF FLUNKEY. The Ambassador from Spain!

AMBASSADOR FROM SPAIN. *(Handing over his carriage)* Compliments of Spain. *(The line is repeated by all but the* 4TH FLUNKEY.*)*

CHIEF FLUNKEY. The Minister from Montenegro!

MINISTER FROM MONTENEGRO. *(With carriage)* Compliments of Montenegro! *(Repeated.)*

CHIEF FLUNKEY. The Minister from Lithuania!

MINISTER FROM LITHUANIA. *(With carriage)* Compliments of Lithuania! *(Repeated down the line.)*

MINISTER FROM SCOTLAND. *(Presenting a very small carriage)* Compliments of Scotland! *(Repeated.)*

(MUSIC. COUPLES *come forward.* FLUNKEYS *stand at attention behind them.)*

ALL.
Oh, trumpeter, trumpeter, blow your golden horn!
Oh, trumpeter, trumpeter, blow your golden horn!
A White House baby will very soon be born;
A White House baby will very soon be born!
Blow your horn!

ALL.
    With a hey, nonny nonny, and a ha cha cha!
    With a hey, nonny nonny, and a ha cha cha!
    There's something glorious happening today
    For all the citizens of the U. S. A.
    A White House baby will very soon be born!
    Oh, trumpeter, blow your horn,
    Oh, trumpeter, blow your horn,
    Oh, trumpeter, blow your horn,
    Your golden horn, your golden horn!

(DOCTOR *enters* L.2, *followed by* 2 NURSES.)

ALL.
    Oh, Doctor, Doctor, what's the news, we pray,
    We've waited for your bulletin all day.
DOCTOR.
    The baby of the President and frau
    Will be here almost any minute now.
ALL.
    With a hey, nonny nonny, and a ha cha cha!
    With a hey, nonny nonny, and a ha cha cha!
    Oh, Doctor, here is the one thing we must know.
    We're all of us anxious and we've got to know:
    The baby, is it to be a girl or boy?
    A baby girl or boy?
    A nation's pride and joy!
    We must know whether it's a girl or boy—a girl or boy?
DOCTOR.
    On that matter no one budges,
    For all cases of the sort
    Are decided by the judges
    Of the Supreme Court. (ALL *repeat.*)
CHIEF FLUNKEY. The *Supreme* Court!

(SUPREME COURT JUSTICES *enter from* R.2.)

JUSTICES. *(Entering)*
    We're the one, two, three, four, five, six, seven, eight,
        nine Supreme Court Judges.
ALL.
    With a hey, nonny nonny, and a ha cha cha!
    With a hey, nonny nonny, and a ha cha cha!

(DOCTOR *and* NURSES *exit* L.2.)

ALL.

> About the baby—will it be
> A boy or girl—a he or she?

JUSTICES.

> On that matter no one budges
> For all cases of the sort
> Are decided by the judges
> Of the *Su*preme Court!

ALL.

> Are decided by the judges
> Of the *Su*preme Court!

CHIEF FLUNKEY. The Secretary of Agriculture! *(Enter LIPPMAN R.2.)*

LIPPMAN.

> Oh—the Farmers in the dell,
> The Farmers in the dell,
> They all keep a-asking me:
> A boy or a gel?

JUSTICES.

> On that matter no one budges
> For all cases of the sort
> Are decided by the judges
> Of the *Su*preme Court!

ALL.

> Are decided by the judges
> Of the *Su*preme Court!

CHIEF FLUNKEY. The Secretary of the Navy! *(Enter GIL-HOOLEY R.2.)*

GILHOOLEY.

> All the sailors in the Navy
> Of these great United States,
> Do not eat their bowls of gravy,
> Nor the captains, nor the mates.
> They refuse to jib an anchor,
> Strike a boom or heave a sail,
> Till you've satisfied their hanker:
> Is it female or a male?

JUSTICES.

> On that matter no one budges
> For all cases of the sort
> Are decided by the judges
> Of the *Su*preme Court!

ALL.

> Are decided by the judges
> Of the *Su*preme Court!

CHIEF FLUNKEY. Senator Carver Jones! *(Enter* JONES R.2.*)*
JONES.

> Out on the prairie,
> The cowboys all keep asking of me:
> He or a she—
> She or a he?
> Out on the prairie,
> For baby boy or girl they are keen,
> But they want nothing in between.

JUSTICES.

> On that matter no one budges,
> For all cases of the sort
> Are decided by the judges
> Of the *Su*preme Court!

ALL.

> Are decided by the judges
> Of the *Su*preme Court!

CHIEF FLUNKEY. Senator Robert E. Lyons! *(Enter* LYONS
R.2.*)*
LYONS.

> Way down upon the Swanee River
> Folks are filled with joy,
> But they want to know what will the stork de-
> liver?
> Will it be a girl or boy?

(ALL *come downstage.)*

ALL.

> There's something glorious happening today;
> A baby will be born,
> A baby will be born.
> Oh, trumpeter, trumpeter, blow your golden
> horn!

(At the end of the number, WINTERGREEN, *followed by* FUL-
TON *and* JENKINS, *enter* L.2.*)*

FULTON. Take it easy, Jack! Nothing can happen to her.
WINTERGREEN. I know, but at a time like this—Mary in
there alone— *(A chorus of greeting from* ALL.*)* Oh! Hello!
God, I'm nervous! I'm—anybody got a drink? (EVERY MAN
brings out a flask. WINTERGREEN *takes* FULTON'S.*)* Thanks.
When I think of Mary in there alone— *(Takes a drink)* Well,
I guess it's not going to be so hard for her.
GILHOOLEY. How is Mary?

WINTERGREEN. Oh! Her! Finest little woman in the world! When I think of what she's got to—anybody got a drink? *(The flasks come out again.)* Well, I guess I'd better not mix them. *(Drinks again from* FULTON'S.*)*

MISS BENSON. *(Enters* L.2.*)* Oh, Mr. Wintergreen!

WINTERGREEN. *(Wheeling)* Any news?

MISS BENSON. The baby will be here at any moment. *(An excited buzz from the* CROWD.*)*

WINTERGREEN. Tell 'em I'm ready. (MISS BENSON *exits* L.2.) My God! You hear that? What do I do now? Anybody got a drink?

CHIEF JUSTICE. Gentlemen, duty calls. The baby is now being born. We must decide the sex.

WINTERGREEN. You decide?

CHIEF JUSTICE. We do, sir.

JUSTICES.
> On that matter no one budges,
> For all cases of the sort
> Are decided by the judges
> Of the *S*upreme Court! *(They exit* L.2.*)*

ALL.
> Are decided by the judges
> Of the *S*upreme Court! *(They are off* L.*)*

WINTERGREEN. I shouldn't be drinking at a time like this. *(To* JENKINS *and the* COMMITTEE*)* Here! Take it away! (JENKINS *reaches for the flask;* WINTERGREEN *pulls it away)* Oh, no, you don't. My wife's the finest little woman in the world! And I can lick anybody that says she ain't!

FLUNKEYS. *(Announcing)* The French Ambassador!

WINTERGREEN. Bring him in!

FRENCH AMBASSADOR. *(Entering* R.2*)* Your Excellency! I have another message from France.

WINTERGREEN. Not another nickel!

FRENCH AMBASSADOR. Will you surrender the baby? *(Reaction from the* CROWD.*)*

WINTERGREEN. Never! Give my baby to France and have it eat snails and get ptomaine poisoning! Never!

FRENCH AMBASSADOR. Then, sir, I am instructed to say that with the birth of the child France severs diplomatic relations. *(Another reaction from the* CROWD.*)*

WINTERGREEN. Hurray!

FRENCH AMBASSADOR. And that is not all, sir. I wish furthermore to report— (2 FLUNKEYS *enter* L. *and blow a fanfare on their trumpets. The* SUPREME COURT JUSTICES *re-enter, to the music of one and one-half Chorus of "On That Matter."* WINTERGREEN *returns flask to* FULTON.*)*

JUSTICES. Whereas—

CHIEF JUSTICE. A child has been born to the President of the United States and his consort—

JUSTICES. Whereas—

CHIEF JUSTICE. The Supreme Court of the United States has been called upon to determine the sex of the aforesaid infant—

JUSTICES. Whereas—

CHIEF JUSTICE. By a strict party vote it has been decided that—

JUSTICES. It's a boy! (JUSTICES *exit to Reprise of "On That Matter." The* COMMITTEE *and* GUESTS *press around* WINTERGREEN *to congratulate him.*)

WINTERGREEN. A boy! That makes me a father! Well, thank you. Thank you very much! I certainly am a lucky man! Boy, the cigars! Smoke up, everybody! Here you are! Have a cigar, Frenchy!

FRENCH AMBASSADOR. My thanks, Monsieur. On behalf of France, permit me to offer my felicitations.

WINTERGREEN. Attaboy! Let bygones be bygones! Have another cigar!

FRENCH AMBASSADOR. And permit me also to inform you that France hereby severs diplomatic relations! *(He reaches for the cigar. There is a reaction from* ALL.*)*

WINTERGREEN. *(Closes the humidor with a bang)* Then the hell with you! *(A buzz in the* CROWD.*)*

FRENCH AMBASSADOR. You understand what this means, Monsieur?

WINTERGREEN. I do! It means no smoke! *(Takes back first cigar; puts it in the humidor.)*

FRENCH AMBASSADOR. Precisely. And where there is no smoke there's fire. I am instructed to say, monsieur, that this means that the French government will— *(The* FLUNKEYS *re-enter. Another FANFARE. The* JUSTICES *re-enter, to music as before.)*

JUSTICES. Whereas—

CHIEF JUSTICE. A child has been born to the President of the United States and his consort—

WINTERGREEN. We had that.

CHIEF JUSTICE. But you are having it again, sir. This one is a girl. (ALL *crowd around* WINTERGREEN *to congratulate him again. MUSIC: Reprise of "On That Matter," on which* FLUNKEYS *exit.)*

WINTERGREEN. A girl! That makes me a father *and* a mother. Well, thanks very much, but I don't know about this! Twins! That's a little more than I counted on!

JENKINS. Cigars, sir?

WINTERGREEN. No, the cigarettes this time! A boy *and* a girl! Well!

FRENCH AMBASSADOR.

Oh, I can stand no more,
My temper's getting gingery;
This certainly will lead to war!
This insult added to injury!

ALL.

Oh, he can stand no more,
His temper's getting gingery;
He says that this will lead to war!
This insult added to injury!

FRENCH AMBASSADOR. You realize what you have done, sir? You have taken away from France not one baby, but two! What you have done to Mademoiselle Devereaux! That poor little girl! Where is she? What is she doing? *(Offstage* DIANA *is heard singing "I was the most beautiful blossom.")*

WINTERGREEN. She's still singing. (DIANA *enters* R.2.)

FRENCH AMBASSADOR. My poor motherless one! My sweet blossom of the Souseland!

FLUNKEY. *(Enters* R.2. Announcing) The Vice President of the United States! *(Exits* R.2.)

THROTTLEBOTTOM. *(Enters* R.2, *knitting a baby's sweater)* Is the baby born yet? I just got this finished!

WINTERGREEN. Only one? Where's the other one?

THROTTLEBOTTOM. *(Pulls out second sweater)* I thought something like that might happen.

FRENCH AMBASSADOR. Once and for all, Monsieur, what are you going to do? What are you going to do about Mademoiselle Devereaux and her babies?

WINTERGREEN. Well, she can have her own babies.

DIANA. But I am not married, Monsieur.

WINTERGREEN. What's that got to do with it?

FRENCH AMBASSADOR. Everything. The family has been illegitimate long enough.

WINTERGREEN. Then let her get married!

FRENCH AMBASSADOR. Exactly! But it was agreed, Monsieur, that she was to marry the President of the United States.

WINTERGREEN. But she can't have me. I'm married.

FRENCH AMBASSADOR. Then it is war, sir. *(Reaction from* CROWD.) When the President of the United States fails to fulfil his duty—

WINTERGREEN. That's it! *(A slap of the hands together)* I've got it!

THE COMMITTEE. Got what?

WINTERGREEN. It's in the Constitution! When the President of the United States is unable to fulfil his duties, his obligations are assumed by—

THROTTLEBOTTOM. (Clapping his hands gleefully) The Vice President! I get her!

CHIEF JUSTICE. Article Twelve!

(WARN Curtain.)

FRENCH AMBASSADOR. Monsieur, you are a genius!

THROTTLEBOTTOM. (To WINTERGREEN) I could throw my arms right around your neck!

WINTERGREEN. Oh, no, you don't! Hers!

(WINTERGREEN passes DIANA over to THROTTLEBOTTOM. MU-SIC. TRUMPETERS re-enter. FANFARE.)

WINTERGREEN. Oh, my God!

CHIEF JUSTICE. It's all right. The boys are merely practicing.

(From up L. a huge canopied bed enters, preceded by MISS BENSON, who is carrying two baby blankets, and propelled by 2 FLUNKEYS, with a NURSE riding on each side of the bed, and MARY, propped up on pillows—with a baby in each arm.)

WINTERGREEN.
                Of thee I sing, baby,
                Summer, autumn, winter, spring, baby·
                You're my silver lining,
                You're my sky of blue;
                There's a love light shining,
                All because of you.

ALL.
                Of thee I sing, baby,
                You have got that certain thing, baby;
                Shining star and inspiration,
                Worthy of a mighty nation,
                Of thee I sing!

CURTAIN.

OF THEE I SING

PROPERTY PLOT

2 Brown Curtains for the portals.
Ground cloth.

ACT ONE

Scene I—*The Campaign Parade.*
    Nothing.

Scene II—*The Hotel.*
    1 red carpet.
    1 bed, pillow and spread—R.
    2 straight back chairs—one R., other C. behind table.
    1 armchair—L. of bathroom door.
    1 small table C.
    1 telephone stand—R. of bed.
    1 luggage stand—at foot of bed.
On Table:
    2 white rock bottles.
    1 whiskey bottle with liquid. } On the shelf under
    1 dark whiskey bottle.   } the table.
    3 glasses.
    Ash tray.
    2 cigarettes.
    Playing cards.
    Matches.
On Telephone Stand:
    1 French telephone.
    2 glasses.
    1 whiskey bottle with liquid.
    3 cigarettes.
Off Stage Left:
    1 blue bathroom tumbler—outside L. door.
Off Stage Right:
    5 bath towels.
    1 tray.

On Tray:
 1 waiter's check.
 1 pencil.
 1 plate.
 3 dill pickles—on plate.
 1 glass bowl.
 Cracked ice—in bowl.
 Ice tongs—silver—on ice.
 8 white rock bottles.
 3 coins—FULTON.
 1 empty cigar box—to rap on for door effect.

SCENE III—*Boardwalk in one.*
 Nothing on.
Off Stage Right:
 8 graflex cameras.

SCENE IV.
 2 curved benches—one R.C., the other L.C., downstage.
 1 table—down R. below door.
 1 table—up left above door.
 2 armchairs—against back flat R. and L. of steps.
 1 single chair—by left table.
On Table Right:
 1 plant in pot.
 1 tin corn muffin box.
 Corn muffins in box.
On Table Left:
 1 stenographer's note book.
 1 pencil.
 Some papers.
Off Stage Right:
 2 motion picture cameras with tripods.
On Walls:
 2 shields R. and L. of center opening.
 3 sets of curtains for center opening.

SCENE V—*In front of Madison Square Garden in one.*
 Nothing.

SCENE VI—*In Madison Square Garden.*
 3 strips of red bunting—for platform railing.
 40 folding chairs.
 4 platforms for chairs.
Offstage:
 1 long roll of paper for THROTTLEBOTTOM.

Offstage Left:
   1 wrestling mat.
Offstage Prompt Side:
   1 gong.
   1 megaphone—(emergency for microphone).

SCENE VII—*Moving Picture.*
   Nothing.

SCENE VIII—*The Capitol Steps.*
   34 batons—one-half off R., one-half off L., for CHORUS.
   1 Bible—off R.—for the CHIEF JUSTICE.

ACT TWO

SCENE I—*The White House.*
   1 large double desk—R.C.
   2 high back chairs—behind desk.
   1 large gold arm chair—above R. door.
   4 arm chairs—
      1 below R. door.
      1 above L. door.
      2 left of the double desk.
On the Double Desk:
   1 large blotter—L.C.
   Lots of papers—all along left edge.
   1 French telephone (electrical dept.) L. of blotter.
   1 cigarette box—downstage of blotter.
   Cigarettes in box.
   Ash tray with match stand—by cigarette box.
   Matches—wooden, in box—on ashtray.
   1 stenographer's note book—lower L. corner on papers.
   1 pencil.
   1 stenographer's note book ⎫
                              ⎬ Lower R. corner.
   1 pencil   ⎭
   2 rubber stamps—beyond blotter.
   1 push button—beyond blotter.
On Blotter:
      Fountain pen set.
      Several checks.
      1 telephone bill.
      1 pad.
      2 pencils.
      1 letter opener.
   Some opened business letters.

On right half of desk:
    1 lady's toilet set—5 perfume bottles and 1 atomizer—R.C.
    1 powder jar with puffs—lower R. corner.
    A number of bills—upper R. corner.
    Several business letters—R.C.
    1 pencil—R.C.
    1 silver envelope holder—beyond blotter.
    Envelopes in holder.

On the Walls:
    1 set of gold curtains—center over painted window.
    1 oval picture of George Washington—L. of painted window.
    1 oval picture of Martha Washington R. of painted window.

Offstage Left:
    Several newspaper clippings fastened—for 2D SECRETARY.
    12 folded sheets of white paper } Hand props for
    12 pencils   } REPORTERS.
    3 wrapped packages—for sightseers.
    1 large push button board with long wire—for JENKINS.

SCENE II—*Before the Senate.*
  Offstage Left:
    1 brief case for JENKINS.
    1 bucket, with wet rag and brush, for SCRUBWOMAN.

SCENE III—*The Senate.*
    18 armchairs—up and down L.
    6 platforms for chairs.
    1 bass drum and beater—above rostrum.
    1 high back arm chair—on rostrum.
    1 armchair—on platform below rostrum.
    2 sheets of paper—on rostrum.
    1 SPEAKER'S gavel—on rostrum.
    1 stenographer's note book—on rostrum.
    1 pencil—on rostrum.
    1 gold watch case—for THROTTLEBOTTOM.
    1 platform cover—for platform outside Senate doors if doubled from Act I, Scene IV.

Under the Chairs:
    22 tambourines.
    1 copy of "Life"—under first downstage chair in 2d row for SENATOR FROM MASSACHUSETTS.
    1 roll parchment paper scroll—upstage chair in front row for SENATOR LYONS.

SCENE IV—*Corridor of the White House.*
  1 cigar—hand prop for WINTERGREEN.

SCENE V—*The White House Ballroom.*
  Offstage Left:
    1 canopy bed.
  On Bed:
        1 spread.
        1 pillow.
        1 sheet.
        4 lace pillows.
        2 dolls.
    1 baby blanket—for MISS BENSON.
    1 stethescope—for DOCTOR.
    2 silver whiskey flasks—for FULTON and JENKINS.
  Offstage Right:
    6 large baby carriages.
    1 doll carriage.
    2 cigar humidors.
    Cigars in both humidors.
    3 whiskey flasks—hand props for JONES, LYONS and LIPP-
      MAN.
    2 baby sweaters—one pink, one blue—hand prop for
      THROTTLEBOTTOM.
    Knitting needles in pink baby sweater.
    Cigars before the show as hand props to FULTON, WINTER-
      GREEN, LYONS, JONES and GILHOOLEY.

OF THEE I SING

ELECTRICAL PLOT

6 front arc lamps and Rheostats and frames.
3 balcony pans, 6 spots each—18 spots in all—plugs, connector and cables.
1 moving picture machine complete with converter.
3 sections of foots, cables, plugs and connectors, complete with frames.
4 portal pipes, 6 spots each, 24 spots in all, cables, plugs, connectors.
1st pipe in one—18 spots, frames, cables, plugs, connectors complete.
2 loud speakers.
1 amplifier set complete.
1 microphone with stand.
4 border lights—3 sections each border—12 sections in all —cables, plugs and connector frames complete.
6 bunch lights complete.
1 flash light effect (flood).
2 flash light lamps (effect).
1 dome light complete, with 6-1000 watt lamps, cable, plugs, connector.
2 telephone bells effect practical.
15 election parade signs complete (practical).
36 torches (practical).
4 switchboards.
1 Atlantic City border—1 section—6 lights.

PLUG BOXES
Borders—12 6 way boxes.
1st Pipe—3 6 way boxes.
Portals—4 6 way boxes.
Front Balcony—3 6 way boxes.
Stage—2 4 way boxes.
Dome—1 6 way box.

Atlantic City—1 4 way box.

Foots $\begin{cases} 1 \text{ 4 way box.} \\ 1 \text{ 6 way box.} \end{cases}$

---

6 40-feet length pipe.
1 30-feet length pipe.
1 converter for amplifier.
1 castor box with supplies.
44 hanging irons.
2 stretchers.
1 French telephone—not practical.
6 iris shutters.
18 focusing frames.
18 safety guard frames.

Detail of Moving Picture Machine Dept.
1 Simplex projector, rheostat complete.
1 A.C. motor.
1 rectifier.
2 boxes.
1 speedmeter.
1 work box.
3 reels of films

ACT ONE

SCENE I—*Street Torchlight Parade.*
Blue foots one-quarter up. Dim out on cue.
2 Arc lamps—blue.

SCENE II—*Hotel.*
Foots—Amber, straw and full blue up.
2d border, amber and straw—full.
18 balcony spots—amber—full up.
Telephone bell offstage.

BLACKOUT.

SCENE III—*Atlantic City in one.*
Foots—Blues, amber and straw—full up.
18 spots—1st pipe—amber—full up.
18 balcony spots—amber—full up.
Portal No. 1—P. and OP. sides—amber—full.
2 arcs—straw—flooded.

2 arcs—straw—panelled on GIRLS.
2 arcs—spots.

BLACKOUT.

SCENE IV—*Atlantic City Hotel.*
Foots, blue, amber and straw—full up.
18 spots—1st pipe—amber—full up.
18 balcony spots—amber—full up.
Borders 2-3-4-5—amber and straw—full up.
6 light—500 watt border No. 29 blue—back drop.
1000 watt P. and OP. sides No. 29 blue—back drop.
Bunch in each entrance R. and L. straw and frost.
Portals Nos. 1 and 2—R. and L.—amber—full up.

SCENE V—*Madison Square Garden Exterior in one.*
16 balcony spots—amber—full up.
Foots, blue, amber and straw—full up.
1st pipe—18 spots—amber—full up.
Portal No. 1—R. and L.—amber—full up.

BLACKOUT.

SCENE VI—*In Madison Square Garden.*
Blue foots—¾ up   } Dim out on cue.
Nos. 2-3-4 borders blue ¾ up }
Ring light—center—white—6-1000 watts.
Microphone and loudspeakers   } Work on cue.
Sound records—cheers.   }
4 flashlights back L.—work on cue.
2 hand flashlight lamps—to go on stage on cue.
2 arcs—white—spots on platform.

SCENE VII—*Motion Picture.*

SCENE VIII—*Capitol Steps.*
Foots—blue, amber and straw—full up.
18 balcony spots—amber—full up.
18 spots—1st pipe—full up—amber.
Portals Nos. 1 and 2—R. and L.—amber—full up.
Borders Nos. 2-3-4-5 amber and straw—full up.
1st, 2d and 3d entrances—R. and L. sides—amber bunch.
2 white spots top of 2d portals R. and L.—pointing back
    center—on cue.
3 arcs—straw—flooded.
3 arcs—white—spotted.

ACT TWO

SCENE I—*The White House.*
  Foots, amber and straw and blue—full up.
  18 spots—1st pipe—amber—full up.
  18 balcony spots—amber—full up.
  Portal spots Nos. 1 and 2—R. and L. sides—amber—full up.
  Borders Nos. 2-3—amber and straw—full up.
  Bunch in entrances R. and L.—amber and frost.
  Telephone bell offstage.
 On Cue:
  Balcony spots, both portals, and 1st pipe spots dim down
    and out, leaving WINTERGREEN and MARY in irised
    arc spot alone.

BLACKOUT

SCENE II—*In Front of the Senate.*
  Foots, blue, amber and straw—full up.
  18 spots—1st pipe—amber—full up.
  18 balcony spots—amber—full up.
  Portals #1 & 2— R. and L. sides—amber—full up.
  4 arcs—straw—flooded.

BLACKOUT.

SCENE III—*The Senate.*
  Foots, blue, amber and straw—full up.
  18 balcony spots—amber—full up.
  18 spots, 1st pipe—amber—full up.
  Portals Nos. 1 and 2—R. and L. sides—spots—amber—
    full up.
  Borders—Nos. 2-3-4-5—amber and straw—full up.
  2-1000 watt bunches—amber—R. and L.—on back drop.
  6 arcs.

BLACKOUT.

SCENE IV—*The Corridor of White House in one.*
  Foots, blue, amber and straw—full up.
  18 spots—1st pipe—amber—full up.
  18 balcony spots—amber—full up.
  Portal spots Nos. 1 and 2—R. and L. sides—amber—full
    up.
  Arcs—white—to follow PRINCIPALS.

BLACKOUT.

SCENE V—*The White House Ball Room.*
Foots, blue straw and amber—full up.
18 balcony spots—amber—full up.
18 spots 1st pipe—amber—full up.
Portal spots—Nos. 1 and 2—R. and L. sides—amber—
full up.
Borders Nos. 2-3-4-5—amber and straw—full up.
2d, 3d and 4th entrances—R. and L. sides—amber bunch.

FINALE.

All ambers are bastard Amber or Special Amber 3 71.
Straw color is No. 6.
Blue is No. 33.
Blue on back drop in Act I, Scene IV is No. 29.

OF THEE I SING

CUES

ACT ONE

SCENE I. Street.
    WARN CURTAIN
    HOUSE OUT

    CURTAIN UP on "AH"
        ARCS ON when curtain is up
        Blue foots on
    WARN BLACKOUT when they stamp after 2d time
        round
    BLACKOUT on 6th Ah-ah-ah-ah-
    STREET DROP UP

SCENE II.
    LIGHTS UP when drop is up.
    PHONE "I brought you some towels." (1 ring)
    WARN PHONE FULTON's entrance.
    PHONE "This fellow lost (laugh—) (1 ring)
    WARN BLACKOUT "A hundred million hearts beat as
        one."
    BLACKOUT—"A thousand words on love tomorrow
        morning."

SCENE III.
    BEACH DROP DOWN
    LIGHTS UP end of 2d phrase in music.
    WARN BLACKOUT when BOYS exit.
    BLACKOUT—GIRLS exit followed by JENKINS. Out **as**
        he exits. Ignore music.
    BEACH DROP UP

SCENE IV
    LIGHTS UP when drop is up.

111

WARN CLOSE IN CURTAIN—Middle of counter-melody (when COMMITTEE samples muffins).

CLOSE IN "Let's all rejoice"

SCENE V

DROP DOWN (Madison Square Garden)

OPEN DRAPES 3d bar of introduction (When 4th BANDSMAN is on)

BLACKOUT AND CLOSE IN WARNING—When GIRLS exit L.

BLACKOUT AND CLOSE IN as JENKINS and BENSON exit L. (Ignore music)

STAGE LIGHTS UP

DROP UP.

SCENE VI

OPEN DRAPES at once.

N.B.—CROWD cheering record on amplifier works on each cheering cue.

WARN GONG "Versus Max Schmeling, German Champion of the world, for the championship of the world."

ONE GONG "in a match for the world's championship."

EIGHT GONGS—When WRESTLER is thrown.

AMPLIFIER DOWN (Signal to electrician) when FULTON holds up hands.

WARN DIM—"And drew you to me"

DIM (Blue borders out) "Sing the campaign song."

WARN CLOSE IN as CROWD starts down stage.

CLOSE IN (Arcs out) "Of thee I sing" (end of song).

SCREEN DOWN

SCENE VII

SIGNAL MOVIE OPERATOR TO START—When Screen is head high.

OPEN CURTAIN as screen hits stage.

AMPLIFIER UP throughout picture.

WARNING—"Wintergreen casts last four votes."

CLOSE IN—As lion appears.

DROP UP.

LIGHTS ON.

AMPLIFIER OFF

SCENE VIII

OPEN DRAPES just before 3d "Wintergreen for President—" in music.

WARN ELEVATOR—"Here's a kiss for Cinderella"

ELEVATOR "All the innocent and all the shady loves, Oh dinga donga dell. Bride and groom. Their future should be glorious. What a happy—"

WARN CURTAIN—DIANA's exit L. "Be off with you, young woman. He's married to his mate."

CURTAIN—Worthy of a mighty nation "OF THEE I SING"

END OF ENTIRE ACT—

ACT TWO

SCENE I

WARN CURTAIN

HOUSE OUT

STAGE LIGHTS UP

CURTAIN UP—(End of third phrase in music) "Why should we care, life is one long jubilee, so long as I—"

WARN PHONE—GUIDE's speech begins.

PHONE—In the very nick of time (Laugh) (2 rings)

WARN PHONE—You know what Senators are, don't you?"

PHONE—"Good morning, good morning." (As WINTER-GREEN is by chair) (1 ring)

WARN PHONE "Tell the telephone company that this is not my bill"

PHONE "Reopened the Bank of the U.S. by mistake" (Back slap and laugh) (2 rings)

WARN CLOSE IN (Front) After exit of Boys and GIRLS

BLACKOUT WARNING—START GENERAL DIM— WINTERGREEN and MARY alone. On the word "Who cares"—

Who cares

If the sky cares to fall in the sea?

We two together can win out.

Just remember to stick your chin out.

Why—

BUZZ FRONT AGAIN—iris spot down.

—should we care?

Life is one long jubilee.

So long as I—

CLOSE IN SLOWLY

—care for you

And you care for me.

BLACKOUT

CLOSE IN FINISHED
STAGE LIGHTS UP
SENATE DROP DOWN
SCENE II
OPEN DRAW CURTAIN
BLACKOUT AND CLOSE IN WARNING
"What about those messages the President is always
sending to Congress? Who reads those anyway?"
BLACKOUT "Oh, boy, wouldn't I like to know."
CLOSE DRAPES

SCENE III
STAGE LIGHTS UP
SENATE DROP UP
OPEN DRAPES 8 bars of music. (Just before they start
humming)
WARNING BLACKOUT AND CLOSE IN—"Posterity
is just around the corner."
BLACKOUT—"Oom pah, Posterity is just around the
corner, around the cor—ner—" (Third beat of cor-
ner)
CLOSE IN

SCENE IV
STAGE LIGHTS UP
CORRIDOR DROP DOWN
OPEN DRAPES
WARN BLACKOUT—"You'll get no tooth from my
baby"
BLACKOUT—"Next year I make a tour of France. La-
fayette."

SCENE V
DROP UP.
LIGHTS UP when drop is up.
WARN CURTAIN Third trumpet call.
CURTAIN—"Worthy of a mighty nation, of thee I *sing*."
ONE CURTAIN CALL WITHOUT MUSIC
HOUSE LIGHTS.

OF THEE I SING

PUBLICITY THROUGH YOUR LOCAL PAPERS

The press can be an immense help in giving publicity to your productions. In the belief that the best reviews from the New York and other large papers are always interesting to local audiences, and in order to assist you, we are printing below several excerpts from those reviews.

To these we have also added a number of suggested press notes which may be used either as they stand or changed to suit your own ideas and submitted to the local press.

"Funnier than the Government and not nearly so dangerous."
—*New York Times.*

"The happiest and most successful native music-stage lampoon that has thus far come the way of the American theatre."
—*George Jean Nathan.*

"It says the most outrageous things in the most outrageous and funniest way."—*New York Herald-Tribune.*

"The piece is a Washington Merry-Go-Round with a hey nonny nonny and a ha-cha-cha, and it gets funnier and funnier."—*The New Yorker.*

In making the award the Pulitzer Prize Committee said:

"This award may seem unusual, but the play is unusual. Not only is it coherent and well knit enough to class as a play, aside from the music, but it is a biting and true satire on American politics and the public attitude toward them. Its effect on the stage promises to be very considerable, because musical plays are always popular, and by injecting genuine satire and point into them, a very large public is reached. The spirit and style of the play are topical and popular, but of course the work is all the more spontaneous for that, and has a freshness and vitality which are both unusual and admirable. The play is genuine, and it is felt the prize could not serve a better purpose than to recognize such work."

In "Of Thee I Sing," I believe that we discover the happiest and most successful native music-stage lampoon that has thus far come the way of the American theatre. With it, further, I believe that American musical comedy enters at length upon a new, original and independent lease of life. That its genealogical tree betrays traces of the plum juices of the late W. S. Gilbert and certain minor blood strains of the later Charles H. Hoyt is more or less evident, but once the fact is allowed it may quickly be dismissed, for the exhibit is fully able to stand on its own feet and to offer itself in its own authentic light.

The reading of a music-show script imposes upon the library armchair a somewhat different attitude from the reading of a dramatic play. That difference is the same difference that attaches to the mood of theatregoing in the instance of a music-show on the one hand and a dramatic play on the other. In the case of the music-show, a volitional predisposition to light pleasure and even gaiety, a humor for intellect-on-the-loose, a leaning to confetti criticism, are essential. The music-show is not for pundits in their punditical moments but for pundits, if at all, in such rare moments as they think and argue with laughter. I accordingly invite the more sober species of reader to engage this script with his top hat cocked saucily over his mind, with his ear filled with the hint of gay tunes and with his eye made merry by the imagined picture of all the relevant and appropriate clowns in the persons of actors, of madly painted canvas, and of appetizing femininity. Only by so approaching it will he get from it what its authors would wish him to.

A glance backward over the modern American musical stage will disclose it to have followed, with little deviation, routine and rusty tracks. In endless succession that stage has given us the so-called romantic musical comedies with their proud princesses in love with humble naval lieutenants and their humble slaveys cinderellaed by proud princes, the revues with their vaudeville comedians and peafowl ladies, the shows laboriously manufactured out of dull comedies previously displayed on the legitimate stage, and the German and Austrian importations adapted to what has been believed to be the American taste by the insertion into their books of a sufficient number of facetious allusions to Congress, Yonkers and Miss Aimée Semple McPherson. Here and there, there has, occasionally, been a mild effort to break away from the established patterns, but the effort has been so mild that it has come to naught, and what has resulted has been, at bottom, much the same old thing. It remained for the authors of "Of Thee I Sing" two years ago to introduce into this swamp, in the show called "Strike Up the Band," the novel bloom that paved the way for the fuller and more highly perfumed sardonic hothouse that the present show is.

In "Strike Up the Band," a sound brand of broad satire was applied to the American music-show stage of our time. That broad satire, smeared generously upon a slapstick, is now applied again, and very much more thwackingly and amusingly, in "Of Thee I Sing." Pour a couple of cocktails into your sobriety and turn the page. GEORGE JEAN NATHAN.

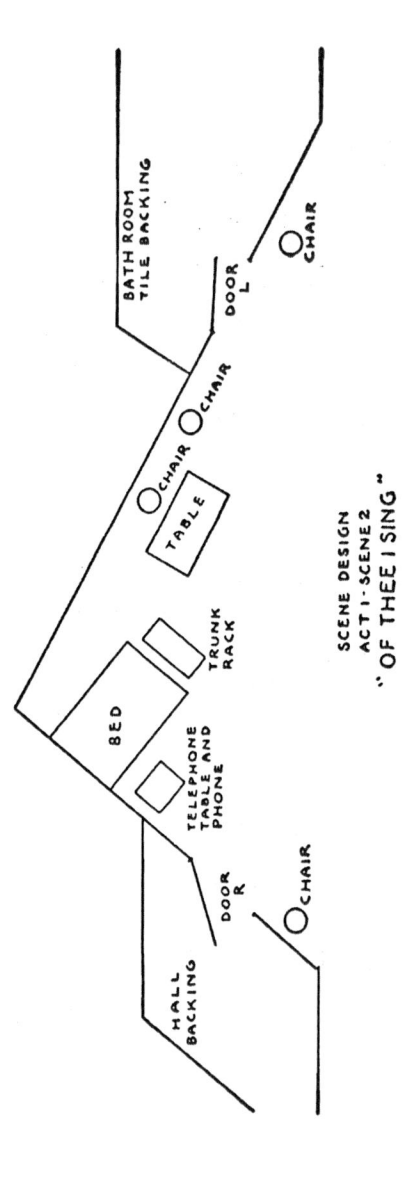

BATH ROOM TILE BACKING

DOOR L

CHAIR

CHAIR

CHAIR

TABLE

TRUNK RACK

BED

TELEPHONE TABLE AND PHONE

DOOR R

CHAIR

HALL BACKING

SCENE DESIGN
ACT I - SCENE 2
" OF THEE I SING "

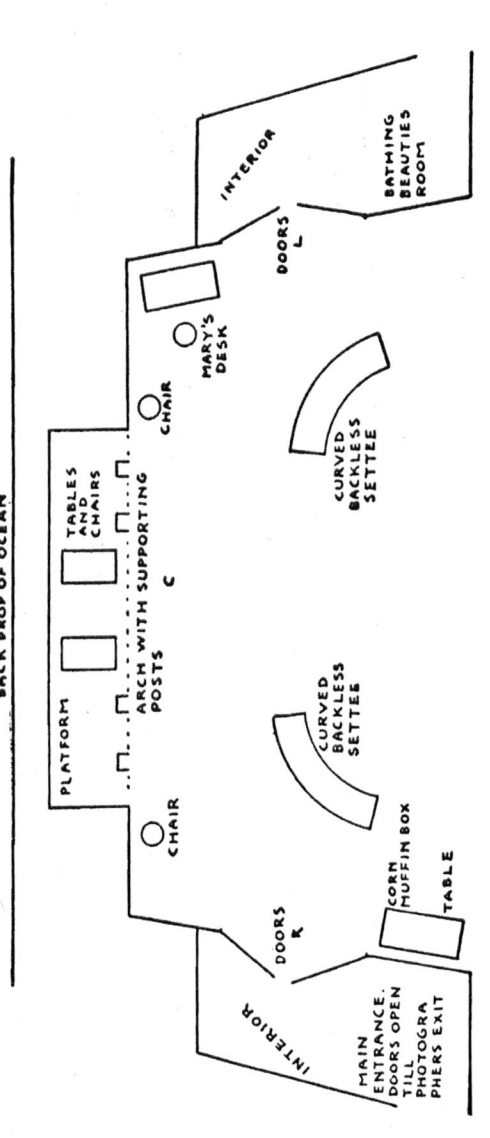

BACK DROP OF OCEAN

INTERIOR

BATHING BEAUTIES ROOM

DOORS L

MARY'S DESK

CHAIR

TABLES AND CHAIRS

PLATFORM

ARCH WITH SUPPORTING POSTS

CURVED BACKLESS SETTEE

CHAIR

CURVED BACKLESS SETTEE

DOORS R

CORN MUFFIN BOX

TABLE

INTERIOR

MAIN ENTRANCE. DOORS OPEN TILL PHOTOGRAPHERS EXIT

SCENE DESIGN
ACT I - SCENE 4
" OF THEE I SING "

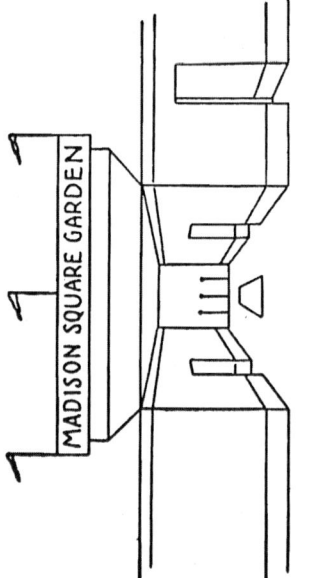

MADISON SQUARE GARDEN

MADISON SQUARE GARDEN
ENTRANCE BACKING

CUTS IN DROP FOR ENTRANCE

SCENE DESIGN
ACT I-SCENE 5
"OF THEE I SING"

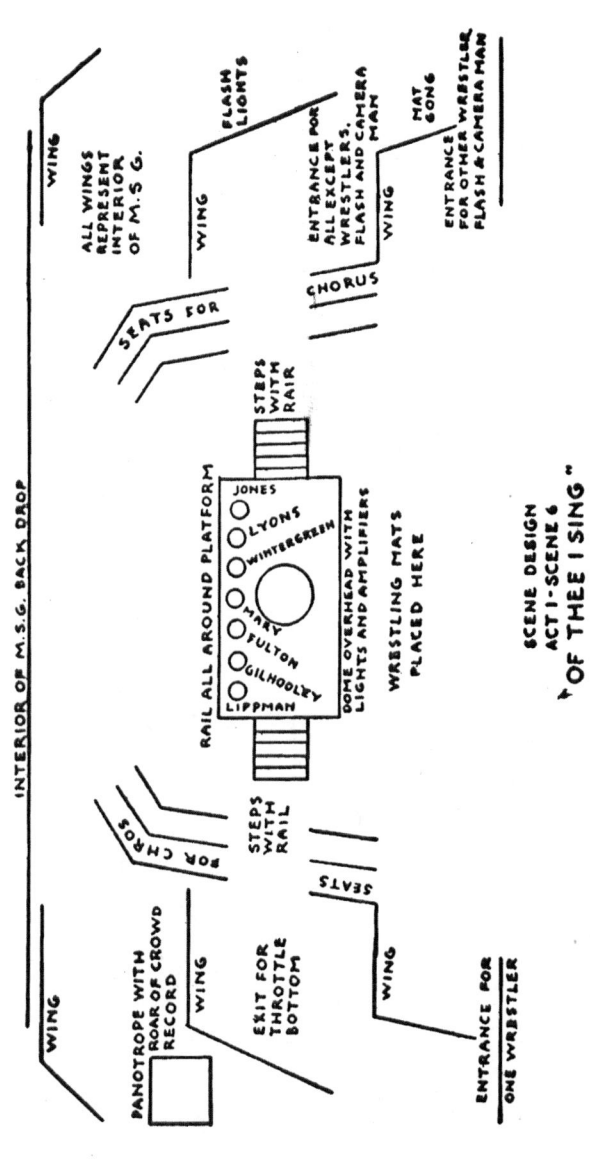

INTERIOR OF M.S.G. BACK DROP

WING

ALL WINGS REPRESENT INTERIOR OF M.S.G.

WING

FLASH LIGHTS

ENTRANCE FOR ALL EXCEPT WRESTLERS, FLASH AND CAMERA MAN

MAT GONG

WING

CHORUS

ENTRANCE FOR OTHER WRESTLER, FLASH & CAMERA MAN

SEATS FOR

STEPS WITH RAIL

RAIL ALL AROUND PLATFORM

JONES
LYONS
WINTERGREEN
MARY
FULTON
GILHOOLEY
LIPPMAN

DOME OVERHEAD WITH LIGHTS AND AMPLIFIERS

WRESTLING MATS PLACED HERE

SCENE DESIGN
ACT I - SCENE 6
"OF THEE I SING"

FOR CHORUS

STEPS WITH RAIL

SEATS

WING

PANOTROPE WITH ROAR OF CROWD RECORD

WING

EXIT FOR THROTTLE BOTTOM

WING

ENTRANCE FOR ONE WRESTLER

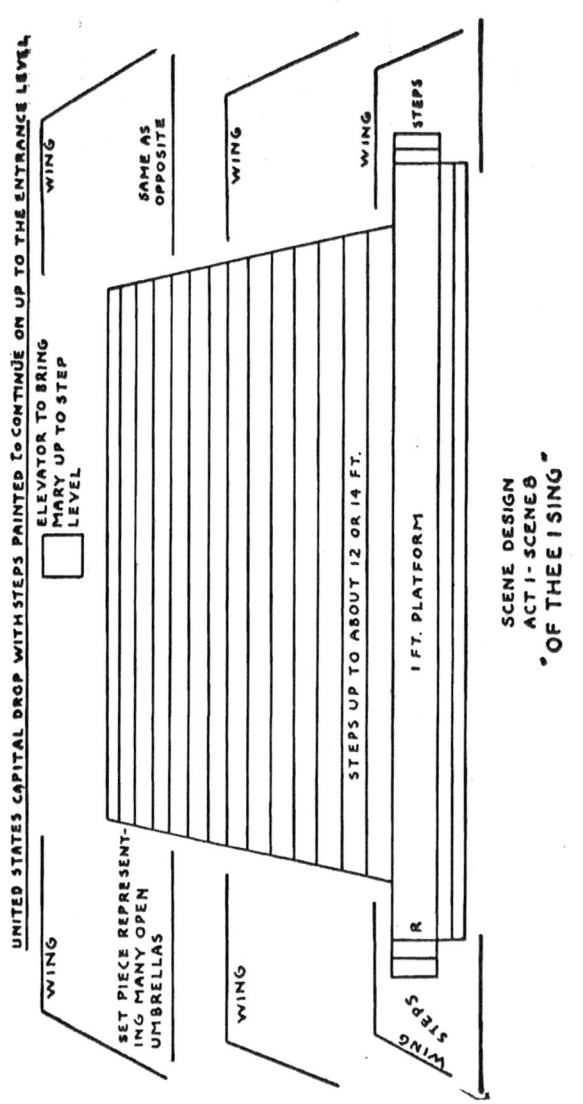

UNITED STATES CAPITAL DROP WITH STEPS PAINTED to CONTINUE ON UP TO THE ENTRANCE LEVEL

WING

ELEVATOR TO BRING MARY UP TO STEP LEVEL

SAME AS OPPOSITE

WING

WING

STEPS

SET PIECE REPRESENTING MANY OPEN UMBRELLAS

STEPS UP TO ABOUT 12 OR 14 FT.

1 FT. PLATFORM

R

WING

WING

STEPS

SCENE DESIGN
ACT I - SCENE 8
"OF THEE I SING"

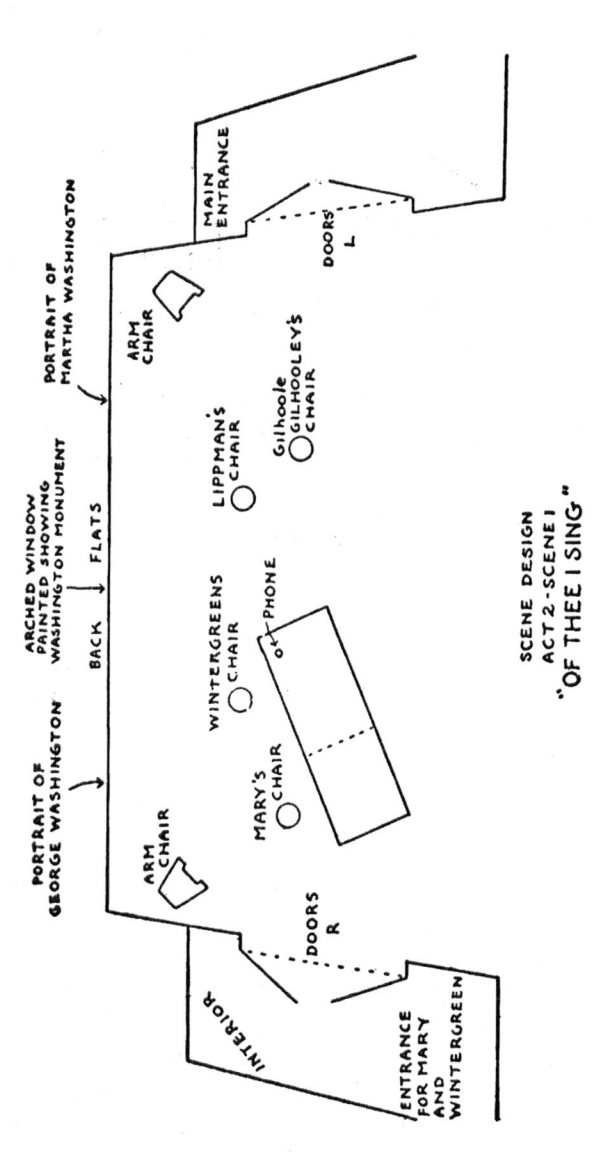

MAIN ENTRANCE

PORTRAIT OF MARTHA WASHINGTON

DOORS L

ARM CHAIR

LIPPMAN'S CHAIR

Gilhoole GILHOOLEY'S CHAIR

ARCHED WINDOW PAINTED SHOWING WASHINGTON MONUMENT

BACK FLATS

WINTERGREENS CHAIR

PHONE

MARY'S CHAIR

PORTRAIT OF GEORGE WASHINGTON

ARM CHAIR

INTERIOR

DOORS R

ENTRANCE FOR MARY AND WINTERGREEN

SCENE DESIGN
ACT 2 - SCENE I
"OF THEE I SING"

INTERIOR BACKING

CLOTH ATTACHED TO DROP SO BACKING GOES UP WITH DROP

DROP OF SENATE

SCENE DESIGN
ACT 2 - SCENE 2
" OF THEE I SING "

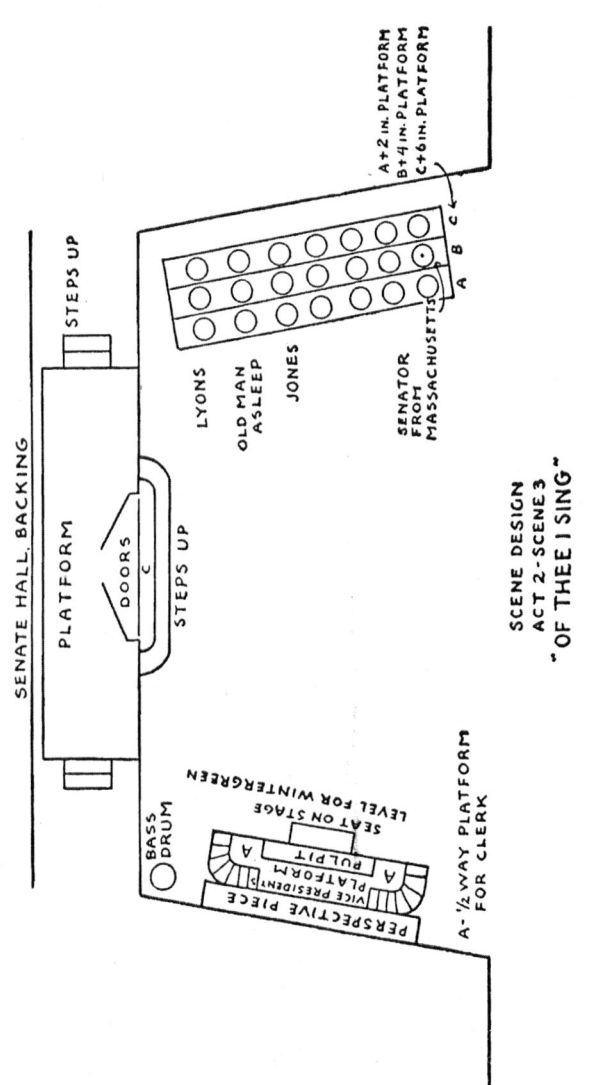

SENATE HALL. BACKING

STEPS UP

PLATFORM

DOORS

STEPS UP

LYONS

OLD MAN ASLEEP

JONES

SENATOR FROM MASSACHUSETTS

A B C

A+2 in. PLATFORM
B+4 in. PLATFORM
C+6 in. PLATFORM

BASS DRUM

PERSPECTIVE PIECE

VICE PRESIDENT'S PLATFORM

PULPIT

A

A

SEAT ON STAGE LEVEL FOR WINTERGREEN

A - 1/2 WAY PLATFORM FOR CLERK

SCENE DESIGN
ACT 2 - SCENE 3
"OF THEE I SING"

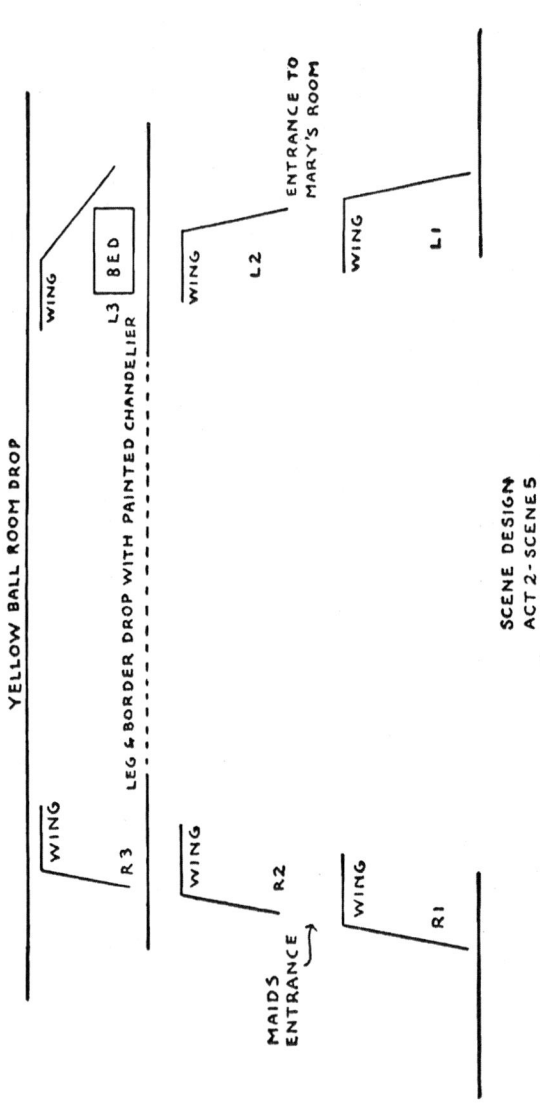

YELLOW BALL ROOM DROP

WING   R3   LEG & BORDER DROP WITH PAINTED CHANDELIER   L3   BED   WING

WING   R2   MAIDS ENTRANCE   WING   L2   ENTRANCE TO MARY'S ROOM

WING   R1   WING   L1

SCENE DESIGN
ACT 2 - SCENE 5
"OF THEE I SING"

OTHER TITLES AVAILABLE FROM SAMUEL FRENCH

SULLIVAN & GILBERT
Ken Ludwig

Musical Play / 8m, 4f / Various interiors or unit set
This clever show takes place at the Savoy Theatre in 1890. Gilbert and Sullivan, who have been feuding for years, are forced to work together one more time: Queen Victoria commands a performance of their most popular songs. Part docu-drama, part period comedy, and part "Gilbert and Sullivan's Greatest Hits," this is a delightful revue from the author of *Lend Me a Tenor, Leading Ladies,* and *Moon Over Buffalo.*

"A charming show."
– *Boston Globe*

"A warm, and affectionate behind the scenes look at this tempestuous, hilarious relationship."
– *Middlesex News*

OTHER TITLES AVAILABLE FROM SAMUEL FRENCH

COLE
Devised by Benny Green and Alan Strachan

Musical / 5m, 5f
Here's a fresh musical about the King of Musicals, Cole Porter. Green and Strachan have cleverly put together most of Cole's hit tunes with a narration that tells the story of his life, from Yale to Paris to Manhattan to Broadway to Hollywood– and, ultimately, back once again to Broadway. Includes such Porter standards as "I Love Paris," "Take Me Back to Manhattan," "Love for Sale," "Night and Day," and "I Get a Kick Out of You." A London success, this delightful new show may be done very simply on an almost bare stage with projections.